Risk Dollarisation®

REDUCED DAMAGE COT = 1NCREA$ED PROF1TS

I0131647

J L Hamilton

Disclaimer

All the information, techniques, skills and concepts contained within this publication are of the nature of general comment only, and are not in any way recommended as individual advice.

The intent is to offer a variety of information to provide a wider range of choices now and in the future, recognising that we all have widely diverse circumstances and viewpoints.

Should any reader choose to make use of the information herein, this is their decision, and the author and publisher/s do not assume any responsibilities whatsoever under any conditions or circumstances.

The author does not take responsibility for the business, financial, personal or other success, results or fulfilment upon the readers' decision to use this information.

It is recommended that the reader obtain their own independent advice.

Dedicated to
Those who think compliance is the dark side
Let us create more profit and less harm
Then we can call ourselves social capitalists!

TABLE OF CONTENTS

Foreword

Personally, I am a socialist. This means that I would, in an ideal world, prefer that all decisions about work and life were made with the interests of human beings as first and foremost. However, I am also a realist and recognise that we live in a capitalist system. In the capitalist system, business decisions are primarily founded on an analysis of financial benefits.

The safety profession has built a discipline on the basis of the moral imperative of minimising the harm to people caused by the workplace. This is a very sound ethical position and serves to motivate a significant sector of the workforce. The natural result of this line of thinking is an approach to safety that emphasises the creation of safety cultures based on values and leadership. In this model, the moral imperative is used to drive the activity of stakeholders in the business.

This model, whilst quite appealing to the rank and file, tends to be at odds with the way that organisations conduct their decision making. In general, organisations are mainly focused on financial outcomes and the related threats and opportunities.

So what does this mean for the safety profession? We are currently at a crossroads: in recognising that the current safety culture and leadership paradigm does not neatly match the current way business leaders think; we have choices. We can either continue to try to convince business leaders to think differently about safety, or we can create a discourse on safety that aligns to the language that business is accustomed to using for planning and decisions.

Let me be clear: I believe it's vital that we create this financially savvy safety approach precisely because I care deeply about minimising the harm caused to people by work and I know that a pragmatic approach to effectively translating safety risk into terms that business and financial people can understand has the best possible chance of delivering that outcome.

It's time for us to recognise that different factors motivate different stakeholders in a business. As an employee, my own health and wellbeing, and that of those around me, is a direct impact. As a CEO or CFO, my entire focus for work is the success of my business.

In understanding this, a realignment in approach can mean that workplace safety and wellbeing gets a seat at the table, and speaking a language that is understood.

If we fail to see the importance of translating our message, we will forever be relegated to referring to threats of noncompliance or moral imperatives, and will miss the opportunity to explain the real costs of getting safety wrong and the benefits of getting it right.

Introduction

Multimillion-dollar businesses around the world are losing millions and they don't even know it.

In fact, the business you're managing right now could be losing millions without you realising it!

You're probably sitting there thinking, how could this be? And then you might try to rationalise why and how this is occurring before beginning to wonder: how do I stop it? This is what this book is about.

Damage Costs are the costs incurred by a business when they incur a damage due to the loss or harm resulting from injury to person, property, or reputation.

The word "damage" is chosen and used to speak to the commercial/business/operational parties of a business whom regularly speak in these terms for stock and sales worldwide.

Damage Costs normally emerge out of areas of business that are deemed to be of Non-Financial Risk; ones that are not normally managed in monetary method or financially reported on, for example, operational risk, compliance risk, conduct risk, IT risk, cyber risk and third-party risk.

This is the area on which we are going to focus.

In the beginning, we found a business that was suffering so many Damage Costs, that they actually contemplated shutting down an entire arm of their business. The business was facing costs of operation specifically around their workers compensation premiums, which were so great that they had considered simply not doing business in an entire state of a country. The usual cost of operation for workers insurance was 6.5%. However, due to high workers compensation premiums, they were paying 16.25%. They operated in a low margin environment with many competitors and this cost meant any margin they had for their work would be lost in this cost alone.

This was clearly a low point. But from crisis, create opportunity. The business found Manage Damage and since then they have been successful in all the states in which they operate.

This is a business that was successful and had sustainable growth, but had not seen this Damage Cost until it was far too late.

Other businesses we have met were internationally listed but were losing millions of dollars in Damage Costs and, due to their accounting structures, were simply unaware. The only reason they knew there was an issue was that their contingency fund pool was getting lower and lower over the years. However, they were not sure exactly why.

We often find that the businesses we help solve the problem of Damage Costs were not even aware of how much they were paying. More importantly, they were not aware that what they were paying was far too much.

The bright side is that, as soon as you uncover your business Damage Costs, this almost directly leads to an opportunity for more profit.

Hearing this, as a business leader, you immediately ask yourself what is possible with increased profit. I'm sure the answer is already on your tongue and you are eager to put those ideas into play.

First, however, you need to know where your Damage Costs are. As soon as we tell a CEO, CFO or COO that they are losing money in a particular area, they race to address it.

Imagine if you could reduce your costs and improve the safety of your employees at the same time?

Risk Dollarisation® is designed specifically to show you how to do this. Risk Dollarisation® is The Financial Approach to Non-Financial Risk.

We believe that, in the future, the Damage Costs of a business are going to be more important. This will occur as we change the way we work and move towards informal work practices, such as the gig economy, more contractors, and as the tides shift towards more automation. Businesses are going to be facing increasing risk of Damage Costs and associated insurances. This will drive up your costs of operations and will most certainly be an area in which the best opportunities can be gained if harnessed appropriately.

In this book, we will also explore the challenges that businesses currently face worldwide.

The Challenge: Non-Financial Risk is not Financially Valued

We discuss:

- What happens when you ignore it?
  - o We show the imminent risks and opportunity for your business;
- What happens if you cost Non-Financial Risk and show you how it helps benefit the business?
  - o We can show you quantifiable, exactable, impartial and factual results
- How can you mark, measure and manage Non-Financial Risk as a budget line item?
  - o We can show you how to appropriately mark, measure and manage Non-Financial Risks in a way that has positive results for workers and your business bottom line.

By the end of this book, you will have an understanding of Risk Dollarisation® that will empower you to take control of your Damage Costs and associated risks in your business.

CHAPTER 1

MONEY TALKS

"Money speaks sense in a language all nations understand"

APHRA BEHN

Safety has Never Been Truly Costed

Safety has never been truly costed; The Risk Dollarisation® Approach where Non-Financial Risk is approached from a Financial Perspective is a new approach for Workplace Occupational Health and Safety.

Non-Financial Risk is those items of risk that are not normally managed in monetary method or financially reported on; for example Operational Risk, Compliance Risk, Conduct Risk, IT Risk, Cyber Risk and Third- Party Risk.

Manage Damage apply Risk Dollarisation® to all these aspects but in this book will explore Risk Dollarisation® for Safety Risk.

In the past, safety has been approached from a number of points of view. In the last twenty to thirty years, the sociological or psychological perspective has dominated approaches to safety.

As it relates to workplace safety, sociology is the study of groups of people (society as a whole) and psychology is the study of the individual within the group.

The table below reflects a selection of past workplace safety approaches, theories and applications. As you can see from the table, many of the approaches have been from the sociological or psychological perspective.

Herbert W Heinrich	Frank E. Bird Jr	Karl' Weick	Thomas Krause	Dupont STOP	James Reason	Patrick Hudson	Dianne Vaughan	Scott Geller	Myers	Andrew Hopkins	Sidney Dekker	Robert Long	Jillian Hamilton
1931	1970	1979-2011	1979 - 1990	1987	1990	1994-2000	1996	2001	2003	2008	2010	2012	2017
Data	Mathematics	Psychology	Psychology	Psychology	Ergonomics	Psychology	Sociology	Psychology	Psychology	Sociology	Safety/Arts/ Science	Sociology	Safety/ Economics
Insurance Data & Statistical Analysis	Insurance Data & Mathematic Ratio Predictions	Organisational Theorist High Reliability Organisations HROs	The Working Interface Measuring Performance Behaviour Based Safety Culture	Safety Training Observation Plan Behaviour Based Safety Culture	Design Human Error ICAM Swiss Cheese	Behaviour Based Safety Culture	Deviance in organisations Social Normalisation of deviance	Selling Idea of Safety Total Safety Culture Behaviour Based Safety Culture	Accidents triggered by unsafe behaviours Behaviour Based Safety Culture	Process Safety Training	Human Factors Safety Differently Safety Anarchy Empowered People	Social Psychology of risk	Risk Dollarisation® Financial Approach to Non-Financial Risk Insurance Data & Damage Costs Statistical Analysis

Manage Damage have found that this approach does not appeal to all people at a business in particular the leaders and managers who are focused on financial outcomes, related threats and opportunities.

We have found a middle ground, a place where we can improve your businesses profits and also improve Workplace Health and Safety. This is a win-win situation and I believe the very essence of Corporate Social Responsibility and the future of business.

In the safety conversation, there is a sincere discomfort about discussing financial costs and workers in one sentence. There is always the position of "how can you put a value on a human life?".

In the other parts of the safety conversation, safety professionals are very comfortable discussing how much you can be fined as a leader for not meeting your duties as an officer. Prior to an event like an incident or workplace illness, this is a very comfortable conversation, one I'm sure you have had or been informed of by your safety professional.

Another part of the safety conversation that safety professionals are also well versed in is reporting on the magnitude of devastation, whereby the cost of a workplace incident is plastered on every newspaper, on TV and in the newsfeed on everyone's phone.

At Manage Damage, we think that businesses are missing an opportunity to capture the costs of damage as they would any other item of business. Widening the conversation around business costs to everyday activities means you can start to manage safety risk like you would any other costs in your business.

Let's be clear: This approach is not about valuing or devaluing workers or humans and human life. This is about revaluing and valuation of an aspect of business that suffers due to a complete lack of cognitive discussion and a lack of the acumen that is applied to all other parts of a business.

Let's also be clear that each person who works at a business is valued. Today, you are costed at your business and you are part of a line item in a budget (plus certain salary, tax, pensions/superannuation and insurance components that are paid).

At Manage Damage, we think that, if you don't treat safety and other Non-Financial Risks like you would any other costs in a business, you lose the opportunity to manage these costs like you would any other.

Money talks: when you start talking about the costs of safety, people listen. They listen when it is in the newspaper, that is, when it's far too late. Let's capture attention before incidents and workplace disasters. Let's follow the money and listen to where our business risk truly lies.

The very essence of news is drama and horror, so we know the price of a catastrophic incident that makes Facebook, Twitter and other newsfeeds.

At the point of no return, when it's far too late, we all start to talk boldly about the incident. We are suddenly openly in a discourse that is even more distasteful because we didn't do enough at the time. It is only when an incident makes the front page that it becomes a requirement to place a value on the cost of safety, due to the damage and devastation that has occurred.

Workplace incidents occur on a daily basis. 7,616 people die every day at work according to the International Labour Organization (ILO), with 2.78 million people dying at work each year. And these are just the reported incidents.

The table below discusses some of the large-scale incidents that have recently occurred at some workplaces around the globe.

The Grenfell Tower fire broke out on 14 June 2017 in the 24-storey Grenfell Tower block of flats in North Kensington, West London, United Kingdom. It caused 72 deaths, including two who later died in hospital. Over 70 others were injured and 223 people escaped.

The Grenfell Tower blaze, Britain's deadliest on domestic premises since World War II, this was social housing provided to those less fortunate by the state.

The fire started just before 1:00am (local time) on June 14, 2017, in the kitchen of a flat on the fourth floor, likely in a faulty refrigerator. It broke out of that apartment, ignited the cladding around the outside of the building, and reached the 23rd floor within half an hour.

In Australia in October 2016, four people lost their lives in an accident at Dreamworld, situated at the Gold Coast. The loss of life was devastating but, as the Inquiry heard, there had been similar incidents prior to the catastrophic event.

The cost of this damage has been estimated as a loss of US$691 million as the company's share prices were impacted by the event and the resultant board reactions.

The cost of damages on share prices alone were high and were prominently covered in newspapers. However, if the workplace had followed those costs that had previously been incurred by the business and had linked each event and their costs to the risks that were posed, then the business may have been able to avoid these fatalities.

In 2013 a factory collapsed in Rana, Bangladesh caused the loss of 1,135 people, one of the largest industrial incidents ever. The cost focus was high for all of the business people involved. The salary of a Bangladeshi working at that factory was about US$68 per month and the factory sold to international design houses. It collapsed and then caught fire because the building itself was not designed to hold so many people and so much machinery. The day before the incident, workers reported to the factory owner that there were cracks in the building. They were told to continue work or risk losing their jobs. The next day there were more than 1,000 people dead and more than 3,000 injured. The factory owner and the clothing buyers, the clients, focused on the cost. This resulted in the factory closing and now the ILO is assisting the recovery of US$40 million in compensation for the workers. This is a very small amount, considering that, if this were to happen in NSW Australia in 2015, for example, the payment for a fatality to a dependant could be AUS$903,639 (US$672,558). That equates to US$763 million for a worker who passed away and on average AUS$11,900 (US$26.6 million) for injured workers. That's a total of US$789.6 million incurred as a result of a business ignoring the risk in the business.

Deepwater Horizon was an ultra-deepwater, dynamically positioned, semi-submersible offshore drilling rig owned by Transocean. On 20 April 2010, while drilling at the Macondo Prospect, an uncontrollable blowout caused an explosion on the rig that killed 11 crewmen and ignited a fireball visible from 40 miles (64 km) away. The fire was inextinguishable and, two days later, on 22 April, the Horizon sank, leaving the well gushing at the seabed and causing the largest oil spill in U.S. waters.

At the time of the explosion, there were 126 crew on board; seven were employees of BP, 79 of Transocean, there were also employees of various other companies involved in the operation of the rig, including Anadarko, Halliburton and M-I SWACO. Eleven workers were presumed killed in the initial explosion. The rig was evacuated, with injured workers airlifted to medical facilities. After approximately 36 hours, Deepwater Horizon sank on 22 April 2010. The remains of the rig were located resting on the seafloor approximately 5,000 ft (1,500 m) deep at that location, and about 1,300 ft (400 m) (quarter of a mile) northwest of the well.

Deep Water Horizon resulted in a loss of 11 peoples' lives and US$61.6 billion before tax.

Society knows the costs of the damage and the impact of lost lives and livelihoods of such incidents. Businesses need to adjust to reflect this knowledge.

Year	Damage Event	Country	Event	People Fatalities
14 June 2017	**Grenfell**	United Kingdom	Building Fire	72
$ Impact (US$) • Council Rehousing Cost US$311.3M • UK Gov't – Replace Cladding - $77.5M • 14 June 2017 - 15 February 2018, RBKC spent £20.9m on rooms at 53 hotels for former residents of Grenfell Tower and evacuees from the Lancaster West estate.				
2017	**Dreamworld Theme Park**	Australia	Ride Mechanical Failure	4
$ Impact (US$) • Company Valuation of Loss ↓43% US$691M Ardent Leisure • Share price from 2.67 – 1.52				
2013	**Rana Plaza**	Bangladesh	Factory Fire & Collapse	1135 fatalities
$ Impact (US$) • A further 3600 suffered or were injured • Primark Bonmarché, El Corte Inglés, Inditex, Mango, Mascot, Premier Clothing and Loblaw Clothing Manufacturer • US$40M to be gathered by ILO where workers are paid US$68/month				
2010	**Deep Water Horizon**	United States	Explosion & Spill	11
$ Impact (US$) • Company Total Cost $61.6B (pre-tax)				

MANAGE DAMAGE

At Manage Damage, we believe: "That which is not valued, is not valued".

Imagine if you and everyone else at your business were given a company credit card at the beginning of the year with no rules, no limitations, no requirements for receipts, no reconciliations, no strategy on costs you could assign, no one specifically responsible and no one checking it until the end of the financial year.

There is a very high probability that the business is going to be looking at a significantly large bill; you would think this would be uncontrollable.

We also know that, if you had this experience last year and there was no intervention, then the experience this year will be the same or worse than the previous year.

Unfortunately, this is how safety and other Non-Financial Risk are approached in businesses worldwide.

It doesn't make sense.

Manage Damage thinks that we must help business leaders understand the value of safety and other Non-Financial Risks.

The reason we created Risk Dollarisation® is that "value" is a subjective amount unless listed and people have different views on the "value" of safety.

We have applied a simple commercial approach to this novel valuation, which means that safety can now be properly costed in the universal language of business.

Money is the Universal Language of Business

Money is the universal language of business and living. We all know the value of a dollar, rupee, euro or krona.

In 1681, Aphra Behn in The Rover stated:

> … Money speaks sense in a Language all Nations understand…

Aphra was right, for the undisputable reason that, no matter what nation, no matter what language you speak, money and its value is a universal language.

Money speaks to people globally.

We have applied a simple commercial approach to the Valuation of Risk Dollarisation®. We'll leave the philosophers and other theorists in safety/risk management to argue over price and value.

Instead, we simply take the costs of input and outputs that relate to Non-Financial Risk and appropriately mark, measure and manage those items.

Money and costs are the universal language for businesses and operations; but only a few safety professionals are speaking about money and cost in safety.

It's time to place an appropriate value on safety. It's time for our professionals whom manage these areas to begin to learn the language of businesses globally. Currently, safety professionals and other non-financial professionals are not involved in the day-to-day operational costs, budgetary assignments or cost assignments of a business. Therefore, many safety professionals are not aware of the costs of operations and they have not been given access to the workers compensation insurance premiums data. They have limited financial acumen because businesses don't support this or require it of them.

Risk Dollarisation® easily translates worldwide. We find this approach is helpful for businesses that operate in a single country or globally.

- Dolarização do risco
- Dolarización del riesgo
- リスクのドル化
- Risk Dollarization
- Dollarisation des risques
- Risico-Dollarisering
- 风险 货币化

Risk Dollarisation® is a true quantifiable measure of a part of your business that has not been managed in this way before.

We know that the insurance market has been valuing your risk and safety for years.

Now it's time to begin managing safety risk in a real way.

This will allow your business to be truly compared to your competitors and allow a real dollar review of your performances year on year.

We must use money terms to define and value safety in order to improve safety and its performance in your business.

The Risk and Opportunity of Money

The monetary approach to risk and safety has vast opportunities for your business.

We find that money is very hard to devalue.

Costs are costs: a dollar used in Part A of a business, if moved to Part B, must be justified and reviewed. The simple disappearance of that dollar is somewhat more problematic for an accountant or finance person in your business.

We know that, in business, sometimes particular incidents are "disappeared" from the records for statistics and reports. It's a form of business magic that transpires as we justify that "this" was work related or not work related or "that" was a non-statistical incident. The very art of safety measurement in today's terms globally is problematic. Many scholars have addressed this issue and we agree that it is done poorly. Apples are being compared with bananas every day. However, we also know that you cannot hide or magically "disappear" the cost of an incident: the business will incur this cost regardless.

It's time to take account of your risk, your real risk, and make a keen and attuned strategy to manage safety in your business.

The very assignment of costs to risk and safety is new, but managing the costs of all other items on your business is not new, so there is a basis from which to start. However, you must not use Risk Dollarisation® and the costs of incidents in the same way that you currently report safety, that is, on billboards out the front of your workplace. Once you take account of your costs and risks in safety, you must ensure a strategic approach to the valuation and addressing of these items to the business.

Just as it is improper or illegal in your workplace policies to talk about a person's salary or how much they paid for their condo or apartment, you should ensure that the costs are discussed in a budgetary sense in the exact same manner as other line items.

The Damage Costs of a business should not be broadcasted on a billboard or shared throughout the entire company, in the way current safety measures are (like TRIFRs and LTIFRs). The information should be shared in a way that doesn't devalue or overvalue the individuals in your team, the workers. We don't want our people to feel like they have been reduced to numbers or dollars.

The information for budgets and business reporting is normally issued down to line managers, and this is where costs of damage and Risk Dollarisation® costs should land.

This is an approach that must be tackled in a manner that aids in lifting the culture within the business to increase the value of safety.

You must also be cognitive if the fact that different generations have different values and approaches to finances. This must be taken into account in your strategic communications for measurement, and through the sharing of information about the success of your Risk Dollarisation® Approach and the reductions in Damage Costs. When you share the success of cost reductions, the conversation to the team must be about the success of reduced injuries, less harm to our workers and future workers, not that we saved US$500k.

Safety and Finance on the Same Team

With Risk Dollarisation®, the safety and finance team are on the same page. In fact, the safety, operations and all business leaders are on the same page, as you are all speaking in the same values and terms when reporting on successes.

This approach sees the financial accountants being a part of safety for the first time. This engagement is profound.

When this occurs, the accountants feel like they are contributing and they begin to also understand the value of safety. Then they start to recognise the reasons for investment in certain items that are normally seen as a constrained procurement.

Increase the Value of Safety

The Risk Dollarisation® Approach increases the value of safety. The historical approach to safety since 1931 has not assigned costs. No value at all has really every been assigned to the safety approach for business.

When no value is assigned, it is either priceless or worthless. Only your personal values and ethics can assign a personal value; when you assign a dollar value, it has a rate to start from and it has been assigned a specific worth.

However, now, for the first time, people can understand what their value of risk in a business is from a dollar perspective.

They can see the value of risk, as related to their previous years' performance, and they can determine aspirations for improvements that are specific, relatable, factual and quantifiable in a form that all parts of a business understand: dollars.

Business People Understand Dollars

Safety is complex. Most safety laws, procedures and processes are layered; they are overlapping and detailed; they can and do go for pages and pages and pages; and business people find them very difficult to understand.

The current safety reporting mechanisms and styles in most businesses use a scale that is completely unrelatable to any other part of a business.

The scores are also cleverly attuned to "statistical and non-statistical", "reportable and non-reportable" and "work-related and non-work related" cases (but somehow work is still paying for it).

With all of these factors in mind, operational and business people can only see trending on increments and declines; other than this, they cannot assign a value that relates to any other parts of the business.

We know that when dollars are assigned, everyone is on the same page and everyone in the business can understand the measurements.

Quantifiable Communication

Business people see, hear and think in numbers all day, every day.

The majority of Non-Financial Risk professionals or safety personnel see, think, hear and act without numbers.

There is a clear cognitive misalignment between financial and non-financial people in a business due to a difference in the way they think. This leads to perceived conflicting goals.

When both parties are conversing in dollars, the language is the same and the message is clear.

True Engagement

Many people struggle with engagement within their safety culture/strategy.

In the 2018 Conference Board CEO C-Suite ChallengeTM Survey, it was noted that engagement was firm on the agenda:

> *"CEOs want to create and maintain an open, safe, and transparent culture..."*

Risk Dollarisation® is a way to firmly engage people about safety. In this circumstance, leaders are now hearing and working within the same language they have been implementing within business for years.

It's not every day you hear an accountant on the end of a phone yell out loud, "WHOOO HOOO!"

This was the reaction of an accountant who worked with the Risk Dollarisation® process. The response came after they received a recovery of insurance payments that was more than they had paid for the whole financial year.

When you can show the value of safety and appropriate risk management in numbers, dollars and business cases, people listen.

By using Risk Dollarisation®, you will gather the hearts, minds and pockets of all of your leaders. This is true engagement and gets even better when you show them the return on their investments.

Safety is Never Costed Until it is Far Too Late

Money is the Universal International Language

Money is a Dirty Word

Safety & Finance on Same Page

Increase the Value of Safety

Business People Understand Dollars

Quantifiable Communication

True Engagement

CHAPTER 2

PROFIT PIPELINE

"A penny saved is a penny earned."

BENJAMIN FRANKLIN

Damage Costs Explained

The use of the term "Damage Costs" to describe your safety risks is a new concept for many developed nations.

The Organisation for Economic Co-operation and Development (OECD) describes Damage Costs as:

> *Damage Cost is the cost incurred by repercussions (effects) of direct environmental impacts (for example, from the emission of pollutants) such as the degradation of land or human-made structures and health effects. In environmental accounting, it is part of the costs borne by economic agents.*

The word "damage" is normally referred to in insurance and legal fields. The Merriam-Webster Dictionary describes it as:

> *"loss or harm resulting from injury to person, property, or reputation".*

It should be noted that the concept is not primarily focused on "damages" in the sense of:

> "compensation in money imposed by law for loss or injury".

Whilst this is included in The Financial Approach to Non-Financial Risk, it is essential that the focus be on avoidance of damage, which in turn results in avoidance of damages in the legal sense.

The word "damage" is chosen and used to speak to the commercial/business/operational parties in a business whom regularly speak in these terms for stock, assets, costs and sales worldwide.

Damage Costs are all of the costs associated with harm in a business environment. "Environment" should be taken broadly, as the OECD has approached it, meaning for the whole operation and the environment in which it operates.

These words and phrases are used to frame a commercial approach to risk and its management in terms business owners know, understand and are comfortable to operate within.

Seek and Discover Unnecessary Damage Costs in Your Business

The Risk Dollarisation® process begins with first seeking and making a discovery of wastage in your business.

The process begins with searching for all of the unnecessary Damage Costs in your business.

Purists would say all Damage Cost is wastage. Ultimately, this is true, as when any production process or system process is reviewed, you will be able to identify and show wastage. The less wastage, the better. And, of course, the lower the wastage and loss, the fewer losses there will be for your business.

The process of finding these costs can take time and should be explored for years gone by.

This is your history of damage. Without knowing your previous history, without reviewing and assessing that data, it will be difficult to inform your strategies for improvement appropriately.

History of Damage in Your Business

Many CEOs, CFOs or leaders in more established businesses today have joined the business many years after its inception.

As a CEO/CFO, you inherit certain aspects of the business, including staff, processes, systems, budgets, profits and more often than not losses: why else would they need a new CEO?

At this point of business entry, you spend time reviewing where the finance balances, how it balances, where it does not balance and then commence strategies to improve the bottom line.

Interestingly, the Damage Costs of a business are not the first, second or third consideration when reviewing a business to identify reasons for losses or ways to improve profitability. The primary focus is on pricing, overheads and productivity. It should also be noted that the traditional accountancy firms do not review this aspect in their audits or merger and acquisition reviews.

Further, Damage Cost histories are never reviewed in a business. However, as a business leader or CEO, if you could review these data sets in dollars, you would gain a clear understanding of your business risks immediately. This kind of reporting would be very helpful for an incoming CEO as they enter a business.

The reason that the Damage Costs are not reviewed is primarily due to the current global approach to safety and other Non-Financial Risks. In this current non-financial approach, they are not costed or budgeted: their elements fall within the current budget lines and are not highlighted as an opportunity for improvement.

Yet these past Damage Costs deliver a clear, succinct way of reviewing safety and other non-financial costs within your business.

Manage Damage have found the identification of Damage Cost values of a business allow a leader to be informed on their business, its past and current transgressions in safety and then, most of all, allows them to be prepared to strategise its future safety business risk.

As a leader, unless you ask specifically, you will not be able to gain these insights.

Even the best accountants, internal and external, find this aspect of business difficult to advise on, as the system is opaque and the reasoning can only be found by review of operations and their impacts to capture the Damage Costs. Generally, they are too removed from operations to be able to provide true advice and strategy.

When you join a business, you inherit the businesses' budget: it becomes yours. You inherit someone else's costs and profits and then become responsible. Our Damage Cost Review allows you to see the past and create a new future.

Your Premium Mirrors Your Performance – Not Only Insurer Prices

Contrary to popular belief (and the occasional insurance calculator change that is economically debilitating), your business premiums and other Damage Costs are a direct reflection of your performance, in the past and today.

You may be told that, "Insurance premiums increased this year", and they may have, but the insurance system allows your business to improve their margins if your business performance, costs and risk profiles improve, even if there was an industry increase across the scheme.

We find that many businesses do not involve the safety/non-financial people when reviewing planning and understanding their Damage Costs.

Businesses, including very large companies, are reluctant to provide these figures or numbers. Even bid managers are sometimes not allowed to know the figures to deliver for tenders!

If you refuse to release these costs and data, which are a direct reflection of your businesses' safety systems, processes and culture, you cannot expect to find the solutions for the damage.

If you do not involve the professionals whom are responsible for managing your damages (and therefore their costs), how can you expect improvements?

They are not being given the whole story and if this history is not shared with them, they cannot undertake the requirements of their job to aid and assist the risk in your business.

The nature of insurance and your Damage Cost is that they are a direct reflection of your risk.

You can influence this reflection by improving your Damage Costs.

Your business may not be aware of how the Damage Costs are calculated, that is, how your business has arrived at certain costs, but this can be navigated easily through a review. Opportunities for improvements will be revealed that can be scheduled, mapped, marked and measured.

Up to 90% Reductions in Some Parts of the World

There are fixed costs to business: tax, payroll tax, super, telecommunications charges and electricity.

We can influence a very small number of the required on-costs or associated costs of business. However, one that is rarely explored is workers insurance.

Your business can gain up to 90% reduction in your Damage Costs within some insurance regimes worldwide. At Manage Damage, we believe that, collectively, business must be globally requesting such incentivised discounts.

Some insurers are passionate about reducing Damage Costs to people. For example, in Queensland, Australia, the state insurer, WorkCover Queensland, offers a 90% reduction on your workers compensation premium for good behaviour. In insurance, good behaviour is low insurance impacts. In essence, if you have a safer workplace with fewer injuries and costs that make it to the insurance claims, then you will be rewarded by paying a lower premium.

What does this look like for a company? As an example, if you have 1,000 staff and the premium you were paying was $960K, your new price could be as low as $96k.

Below is a table showing the benefit that a 90% discount could apply to your business size. Whilst the options for a 90% discount are not yet available in other states of Australia, we are showing it here for two reasons. One, to highlight the value of good safe performance and two, to ask boldly: Why don't the other states offer this kind of reward? In Queensland, an employer with 1,000 staff could pay either A$960k or A$96K for the same service and coverage if the discount is based upon good insurance ratings.

Effects of 90% on Your Business Workers Compensation Premiums 2017FY
Queensland Actual Opportunity - How other States Could Benefit

MANAGE DAMAGE

2016-17	NSW	VIC	QLD	WA	SA	TAS	NT	ACT
Average Premium rate (% of payroll)	1.397	1.272	1.2	1.525	1.8	2	2.33	2.58
10% (% of payroll)	0.140	0.127	0.120	0.153	0.180	0.200	0.233	0.258
50 Staff 100%	55,880	50,880	48,000	61,000	72,000	80,000	93,200	103,200
50 Staff 10%	5,588	5,088	4,800	6,100	7,200	8,000	9,320	10,320
100 Staff 100%	111,760	101,760	96,000	122,000	144,000	160,000	186,400	206,400
100 Staff 10%	11,176	10,176	9,600	12,200	14,400	16,000	18,640	20,640
300 Staff 100%	335,280	305,280	288,000	366,000	432,000	480,000	559,200	619,200
300 Staff 10%	33,528	30,528	28,800	36,600	43,200	48,000	55,920	61,920
500 Staff 100%	558,800	508,800	480,000	610,000	720,000	800,000	932,000	1,032,000
500 Staff 10%	55,880	50,880	48,000	61,000	72,000	80,000	93,200	103,200
1000 Staff 100%	1,117,600	1,017,600	960,000	1,220,000	1,440,000	1,600,000	1,864,000	2,064,000
1000 Staff 10%	111,760	101,760	96,000	122,000	144,000	160,000	186,400	206,400
5000 Staff 100%	5,588,000	5,088,000	4,800,000	6,100,000	7,200,000	8,000,000	9,320,000	10,320,000
5000 Staff 10%	558,800	508,800	480,000	610,000	720,000	800,000	932,000	1,032,000

There are incentives and discounts for Good Behaviour (i.e. lower Damage Costs) in almost all insurance regimes worldwide.

In Canada, the Workers Compensation Insurance Scheme the cost of Workers' Compensation insurance depends upon what industry category your business is in. All schemes classify businesses according to the industry in which they operate, because it's assumed that businesses with similar operations share similar risks.

All WCBs use a performance-based pricing system, which will also affect the cost of your premiums for better or worse. On the positive side, employers who reduce the number of accidents and injuries in their operations pay less. The downside is that employers with poor accident and injury track records pay higher premiums.

This experience plan means that you can earn discounts on your Workers' Compensation insurance premiums over time. Some provinces, such as Alberta, provide even more incentive; you can earn an additional discount of up to 20% by participating in the Partners in Injury Reduction program.

In NZ, the Workers Compensation Insurance Scheme allows discounts where the Work Levy can be reduced by preventing injuries at work and assisting injured employees return to work sooner. If a company has paid less than $10,000 annual Work Levy in any one of the three years, they will fall under the No Claims Discount programme.

Companies will be given a 10% discount on the Work Levy if, over the three-year period the business has had:

- no weekly compensation days, and
- no accidental death claims.

Companies will be given a 10% loading on the Work Levy, if over the three-year period the business has had:

- over 70 weekly compensation days or
- any accidental death claims.

Through the Experience Rating Programme, companies could get up to 50% off the Work Levy or, up to 75% added.

Some systems do not allow performance-based discounts. This is an aspect that Manage Damage questions, as it becomes a socialist approach without reward for good performers and additional costs for bad performers. The whole scheme could, in theory, be paying more due to one bad company causing high costs and injury damages. It is our experience that the incentive to perform better with discounts leads to better performance and that the Risk Dollarisation® approach could lead to improved scheme performance.

In many countries like Germany and Pakistan for example, the Workers Compensation Insurance Scheme does not allow discounts by industry or company performance they just have single flat rates for their insurance. We have had discussions with groups about this approach and the advantage of discounts and tiered pricing with higher price for higher risk and lower prices for lower risk.

Your business has an opportunity to understand these mechanisms so that you can benefit from not only increased profits but also improved safety for your people and the community.

To be clear, whilst workers compensation insurance is one major element of Damage Costs, it is not the only measure. Other damages, such as damage to property, damage to plants, legal costs and other measures, which have been listed previously, are also included.

Damage Cost Black Holes

The way that businesses currently reconcile Damage Costs leaves room for error and creates an environment ripe for Damage Cost black holes.

Damage Cost black holes are those environments where "money apparently disappears without trace".

When you Google, "What would you see if you fell into a Black Hole?", it won't say, "Millions of wasted dollars in Damage Costs". But it should.

This is where your profit goes due to mismanagement of your business's damage and Damage Costs.

Upon review of some business arms or areas, it has been shown that the Damage Costs were far greater than the gross profit and revenue. This is a clearly unsustainable business practice and position.

How could this occur, you ask? It was due to the fact that the "costs" associated with certain areas were not considered to be "their" costs; they were being considered to be other grouped costs for the business, as group overheads. Other parts of that business group were being financially disadvantaged due to one arm of the business. As I mentioned earlier, in one extreme case, it was decided it was better to close that business arm than continue.

Many businesses are unaware of Damage Costs within certain areas in their business. The exercise of finding these costs provides significant insights to the business stakeholders upon review.

Cost it – Then Mark Measure and Manage It

We have found that, once businesses find costs, management is easy. It becomes just like other costs and parts of their business.

This is not rocket science for leaders; it is how they manage all costs business wide. However, because this approach for Damage Costs is new, it can seem a little daunting.

When safety and other Non-Financial Risks are included in the budget, it is done in a very different way that could have significant results. Whenever you cost anything in a business and it becomes a budget line item, it becomes important.

This encourages a new focus on the line item. Simple calculations mean that when you know how much it costs today and how much it should be on average, plus what it cost last year and if it is increasing, then you know that there is work to be done or that the results are good.

Either way, you know where you stand. It is now marked, measured and managed as any other line item on the budget and will be held to account as appropriate.

Budget Returns

The nature of the majority of Damage Costs is under a predictable model or costing scale.

Your workers insurance is normally measured over a period of 3-5 years of business performance. As a result, you can actually budget returns on profits that are reflective of decreased risk and Damage Costs, and therefore schedule premiums.

You can plan for improved Damage Costs, so your actions and strategy can make real, true and accurate results for your business.

We know that, in business, one dollar saved is often like making ten, if your company works on 10% margins.

If you could save $100k on premiums, you have just generated $1 million in "sales".

I know that this sounds appetising to leaders and it should.

It should also sound appealing to the Non-Financial Risk parties in your business as well. Less damage results in these savings. Fewer people are being hurt, so the insurance companies will reward you with discounts accordingly.

This is what you call a win-win situation:

Safety wins and production wins.

In fact, this is one and the same thing!

Damage Costs Explained

Seek and Discover Unnecessary Damage Costs

The History of Damage Costs at Your Business

Your Premiums Mirror Your Performance

Up to 90% Reduction in Some Jurisdictions

Damage Cost Black Holes

Cost It - Then Mark Measure Manage It

Budget Profit Returns

CHAPTER 3

THE NUMBERS DONT LIE

"The numbers don't lie and they spell disaster for you."

SCOTT STEINER

People Tend to be a Little More Creative

In those areas of business where there are no clear, accurate, accounted line items, it is a little easier to be creative with the results.

Non-Financial Risk particularly suffers from this issue, which creates a high error rate.

The way safety reporting is conducted, for example, using Total Recordable and Lost Time Injury Frequency Rates (TRIFRs, LTIFRs) is significantly problematic because, for a damage or risk to be included, it must first be reported.

If the item is not reported, it will not appear in the results of the safety measurement and reporting.

Therefore, non-reporting creates an error. The rate of this error is normally very high, especially if the culture is focused on tender-based work where there are demands for low or zero TRIFRs/LTIFRs. It's simply lower with less reporting.

The second error that occurs is the classification of incidents.

All businesses have "reportable and non-reportable" incidents, "statistical and non-statistical" incidents and "work-related and non-work-related" incidents. We wonder why a business would concern itself with "non-work related incidents" at work, if it wasn't work-related.

So, the error rate is also impacted by classification.

We find that, if you use measurements that are clear, factual and unequivocal, it is difficult to arrive at different outcomes.

Damage Costs are very difficult to "hide", "not-report" or "re-classify" in a business, unless you are putting your hand into your own pocket.

A dollar is a dollar and unless there is a section of a business that is willing to hold Damage Costs that do not align to their budget, then the costs should be clear.

Uncover Damage Costs

When you uncover the specific Damage Costs in particular areas, a whole new business view is taken.

Your view of certain performers who were once seen as high performers with excellent business results can sometimes be altered, as you find that they have high Damage Costs and, subsequently, substandard overall business results.

Performance measures now account for damages and Damage Costs. When the Damage Costs uncovered are specifically assigned to certain business units, the results can be surprising, often in a negative way.

The example below compares what reporting would have looked like for Area A in the most simplistic terms using each method:

Scorecard A for Area A – Pre Damage Costs Reporting	
Time	Better Than Projected
Cost	Below Budget
Quality	Excellent
Safety	Zero LTIFRs

Scorecard A for Area A – Post Damage Costs Reporting	
Time	Better Than Projected
Cost	Above Budget
Quality	Excellent
Safety	Damage Cost Ratio High

Business Systems Hide This Cost

Damage Costs often get lost in business systems.

We find that the larger and more complex a business structure is, the more difficult the Damage Costs are to identify, simply due to the traditional cost allocation methods.

In particular, some costs that are Damage Costs related are even more difficult to assign, as the "confidentiality" of some costs tend to lead to extensive disclosure issues, even internally.

Hidden costs are very hard to manage, whereas transparency of costs leads to excellent financial outcomes and a safer workplace.

Pinpoint the Damage Costs

When you undertake the process of searching for Damage Costs, you begin to find out exactly from where the Damage Costs are coming.

You then have a brand new insight into your incidents, the damaging forces, and the reported and unreported elements become clear.

This allows you to pinpoint when and where your impacts are occurring and then, can inform your strategy to "Manage the Damage".

Regain Control

By undertaking the exercise of exploring your Damage Costs, you get to find out exactly where the Damage Costs are coming from so you can act appropriately.

You can regain oversight of your business and ultimately regain control of costs that often are part of the "Black Hole" section of your budget with limited explanations and even more limited improvement mechanisms.

Known Best Performers/Best Performing Areas are Adjusted

With a new view on your business and the actual Damage Costs in all parts of your business, you can start to adjust your view of the best performing areas according to true costs and real risks.

Regain Margins

When you have this new view and brand new insight into your damages costs and performance areas, you can adjust your actions and strategic implementation to regain your margins.

This process is very successful and will gain dramatic returns for your business.

Adjust Your Returns

When you regain you margins, you can then adjust your current and expected returns.

This process is so powerful. It is very compelling to watch operational people who did not understand the value of safety and the associated Damage Costs turn their ear and eyes to safety. Only then do they understand the true impacts of a safe, efficient, productive and profitable workplace.

People Tend to be a Little More Creative

Uncover Damage Costs

Business Systems Hide This Cost

Pinpoint the Damage Costs

Regain Control

Know Best Performer People & Areas Redefined

Regain Margins

Adjust Your Returns

CHAPTER 4
ROI ON PREVENTION

"Expenditure on Work Reintegration is now 3.7 to 1."

INTERNATIONAL SOCIAL SECURITY ASSOCIATION

Justification for Spending

Business owners need justification for all items spent within a business budget. This is a fact.

There is even more pressure for this justification when there are boards and shareholders to consider. The justification is essential even on the micro-scale for small to medium enterprises, as there is very little room for expenditure that is non-essential.

An explanation must be given regarding the need for the item of expenditure, which must be supported by documentation to show that expected returns exceed expected costs.

If your division, area or department needs to make expenditure, it must justify, account for and warrant this spending. Each division often make a warrant or business case by demonstrating the expected financial returns and expected time frames for each item.

In Non-Financial Risk areas, spending is often performed under "faith", with very few business cases generated.

When asked about their budget, many safety professionals reply, "What budget?", "I don't have a budget", "Safety is essential and I should be able to spend on anything we recommend" or give a vague justification like, "That money's just for our internal safety training and personal protective equipment".

All of these answers make us uncomfortable, as they are all inconsistent with The Financial Approach to Non-Financial Risk.

Justification of expenditure is not just a convincing "Pleeeeezzzee", like you asked your parents for money when you were a teenager.

In business, returns on investment are expected. Business owners must know what they are buying and what the return or benefit of this expenditure will be.

Business owners expect that spreadsheets, numbers and calculations be used, just for a start. So what shouldn't a business case look like?

Spent Thousands/Millions on Safety with Business Case of Hope

We need to reflect on how business cases have been used by your teams in the past and today.

How has or is safety expenditure justified?

- Has the justification been a "Just Because" regime?
- Has it been because someone said, "The Regulator Says", so we must?
- Has it been "The Government Says", so we must?
- Has it been "Safety Simon Says", so we must?

Reflect on your past and current expenditures, and determine if you've accepted spending because you: believe it's a required expenditure based upon your cultural valuation on safety; think that the law/government says you must make that purchase; or have utter faith in Safety Sam/Simon's opinion on what to spend?

Once you've figured this out for each department or item, it's time to shift the approach of everyone making business cases in your company.

Business Case for Expenditure

We know that a clear compelling business case for expenditure is much more compelling; it's much easier to justify and much quicker to be approved.

A clear Damage Cost-Benefit business case shows the clear reasoning for expenditure, the benefit and the returns expected; all in dollars.

When safety Risk and Damage Costs are approached in this manner, people hear and understand what you are seeking.

Your staff's new costed business cases presented in this way will be easily justified to you, your superiors, boards and shareholders.

Feedback on ROI

The normal business routes of expenditure on financial risk involve feedback from your business on the return of investment.

Very often, the loop is not closed with Non-Financial Risk.

The fact is that good expenditure on safety (prevention & return to work) has been proven as a return of 3.7 times in a recent report issued by the International Social Security Association (ISSA) in September 2017.

ISSA Report of Return of Investment for Prevention and Reintegration: Until September 2017, the ROI was found at only 2:1. The report has now confirmed 3.7:1 and we see cases of up to 6:1 at Manage Damage.

This report was a follow-on from a 2013 ISSA report that focused specifically on the return of prevention.

Pakistan also commissioned a report in the same vein: Calculating the Return on Prevention for Companies, Costs and Benefits of Investments in Occupational Safety and Health in Pakistan's Textile and Garment Sector. The report was delivered through collaboration with the Labour and Human Resource Department, the Government of Punjab, the HomeNet Pakistan and Bavarian Employers' Association (Bfz)/ESPIRE project, the German Social Accident Insurance Institution for the Energy, Textile, Electrical and Media Products Sector (BG ETEM), the German Social Accident Insurance (DGUV) and Deutsche Gesellschaft für Internationale Zusammenarbeit (GIZ) GmbH.

Deutsche Gesellschaft für Internationale Zusammenarbeit (GIZ) GmbH are planning to complete more studies, as their work has gained interest worldwide. It has had significant positive impacts for people's safety in some of Pakistan's major businesses.

Amazingly, the return on investment can be even better than the amount quoted above. It can reach up to 6 to 8 times, depending on the Damage Costs and current status when the business is entered for interventions.

The challenge facing non-financial professionals is that the benefit of that expenditure is not fed back to the business in feedback on the ROI.

If the business was operating in a financial approach to Non-Financial Risk, however, this would be required. The value would then be recorded, known, and understood clearly by all parties in the business.

ROI Proved and Shared

When a business shows its ROI and it is proved and shared, they increase the value and worth of safety and other Non-Financial Risks.

Return on investment reporting serves as a standardised metric for measuring the financial efficiency of investment opportunities.

ROI is commonly used and will help describe an opportunity to others, especially those that need convincing that an investment is worthwhile.

The benefit of ROI feedback being captured, proved and shared is extremely powerful in a business leadership team.

Justification for Spending

Expenditure of Thousands with 'Hope Business Cases'

Business Case for Expenditure

Feedback on Return of Investment (ROI)

ROI Proved and Shared

CHAPTER 5
THE COST OF DAMAGE

"He who fails to economize will agonize."

CONFUCIUS

Damage Costs are Unnecessary Profit Losses

Damage Costs are clear unequivocal losses.

Damages costs are a result of error; businesses that aim for low error systems tend to increase profit.

The function of finding Damage Costs is determining what in the system of process is latent, creates time lapses, causes harm and creates damage.

High Damage Costs are a result of poorly managed business systems and processes.

The challenge faced by business leaders is that, if you are not presented with this information, how can you improve it?

Costs Accounted for Specifically

We know that if the leader is shown specifically where the costs are, they can be managed.

It's so simple and then so powerful.

So how can you do this? Some important numbers to take charge of are listed in the table below:

SOME IMPORTANT NUMBERS	
Suitable Duties	Medical
Counsellors	Investigators
Public Liability	Legal
Physiotheraphy	External providers
Doctors	Surveillance
Common Law or Legal Claims	Insurance

This is the starting point for how you can understand your Damage Costs and how you can improve you whole system, reduce error rates and increase your profit.

Thousands/Millions Unaccounted for in The Past

When this exercise is undertaken, and the losses are highlighted and accounted for, it can be very confronting.

It changes a leader's whole perception on how a business is functioning and operating.

This process helps CEOs and CFOs find amounts in the order of thousands and millions of dollars: dollars that were lost and often they were not even aware.

Gazette - Public Available Data

You can view the specific industry averages of performance of a collective group of risk by consulting and reviewing the local industry gazettes and insurance standards.

This means a business owner does not need to imagine what their performance is compared to the rest of industry. The rates listed are the averages or starting rates that have been calculated by actuaries based upon the collective performance of your industry group.

Your Business Should Always Perform on or Below Industry Rates

As a business owner, it is expected that your business will perform better than the Industry: you don't want to be performing in a position where your competitors have an advantage over you.

All businesses should always aim to be operating at below the industry gazette averages.

The margin your business can save/gain instantly compared to your competitors, as discussed before, can be vast.

Let's show you three real scenarios for the same kinds of business, with three very different financial outcomes.

In all scenarios, the baseline is the same for performance of a collective group of risk to an insurer.

Wages: Average $60,000 per worker per annum
Workers: 500 people
Total Wages: 30 million
Average Insurance Rate: 2%

MANAGE DAMAGE

Insurance Scenario	Average Industry Rate Performer	Optimal Performer 90% Discount	Worst Performer (capped 2 x)
Premium Amount	$600k	$60k	$1.2M

I am yet to meet a business owner who would prefer to pay $1.2M for a service that could cost as little as $60k. In this example, the worst performer is paying 1900% more than the best performer!

If your business is paying $1.2M for a workers compensation premium bill and your competitors are paying $60k or $600k, even if we work from the actual industry rate, your business is paying $600k more to operate than one of your direct competitors.

Starting with an overhead that is $600k greater than your competitors is far from optimal.

If you make 10% margins for sale, you are going to have to make $6M in sales to catch your competitor's position.

Below is the position of each business if you and your competitor make $100M in sales each, with a 10% sales margin.

MANAGE DAMAGE

Insurance Scenario	Average Industry Rate Performer	Optimal Performer 90% Discount	Worst Performer (capped 2 x)
Premium Amount	$600	$60k	$1.2M
Sales/Revenue	$10M	$10M	$10M
Margin (10%)	$1M	$1M	$1M
Revenue minus Premium	$400k	$940K	$(200K)

Your business can either have a $940k profit or a $200k loss with all of the same variables except your workers compensation premium.

Here is another example of three variable outcomes for Aged Care Health in Queensland:

Wages: Average $80,000 per worker per annum
Workers: 200 people
Total Wages: 16 million
Average Insurance Rate: 2.557%

MANAGE DAMAGE

Insurance Scenario	Average Industry Rate Performer	Optimal Performer	Worst Performer (capped 2 x)
Premium Amount	$409,120	$40,912	$818,240
Sales/Revenue	$10M	$10M	$10M
Margin (10%)	$1M	$1M	$1M
Revenue minus Premium	$590.9k	$959K	$181.8K

Your business can either have a $959k or a $181.8k profit with all of the same variables except your workers compensation premium.

Your Current Business Costs of Injury and Incidents are Available

It should now be clear that, as a business leader, you should seek out and review your workers compensation premiums.

By reviewing your existing costs, outlays, premiums and valuations, you can find your costs of damage. When you do this, you can start to understand some of your Damage Costs. This will allow you to see how you stand compared to your competitors.

Relativity – Compare Your Costs

The transparency of workers compensation rates most certainly allows you to see how you perform specifically to your competitors and that of the industry averages.

You can directly compare your costs with your industry competitors' costs of damage.

For example, below is a table of the average costs to insure in Australia, New Zealand and Germany, state-wide according to the 17/18FY.

Average Scheme Costs to Insure 2017/18FY

MANAGE DAMAGE

Australian Capital Territory	2.58
Northern Territory	2.33
Tasmania	2
South Australia	1.8
Western Australia	1.525
New South Wales	1.397
Germany	1.3
Victoria	1.272
New Zealand	1.21
Queensland	1.2
Comcare (AustralianPublic Service)	1.14

The Australian and New Zealand industry workers compensation rates per industry area will also show you specific detail about your industry, within the following guidelines.

Each business will operate under a coding system and units within each division; each country has different codings, but will allocate a group under each defined unit.

- DIVISION A: AGRICULTURE, FORESTRY AND FISHING
- DIVISION B: MINING
- DIVISION C: MANUFACTURING
- DIVISION D: ELECTRICITY, GAS, WATER AND WASTE SERVICES
- DIVISION E: CONSTRUCTION
- DIVISION F: WHOLESALE TRADE
- DIVISION G: RETAIL TRADE
- DIVISION H: ACCOMMODATION AND FOOD SERVICES
- DIVISION I: TRANSPORT, POSTAL AND WAREHOUSING
- DIVISION J: INFORMATION MEDIA AND TELECOMMUNICATIONS
- DIVISION K: FINANCIAL AND INSURANCE SERVICES
- DIVISION L: RENTAL, HIRING AND REAL ESTATE SERVICES
- DIVISION M: PROFESSIONAL, SCIENTIFIC AND TECHNICAL SERVICES

  – DIVISION N: ADMINISTRATIVE AND SUPPORT SERVICES

  – DIVISION O: PUBLIC ADMINISTRATION AND SAFETY

  – DIVISION P: EDUCATION AND TRAINING

  – DIVISION Q: HEALTH CARE AND SOCIAL ASSISTANCE

  – DIVISION R: ARTS AND RECREATION SERVICES

  – DIVISION S: OTHER SERVICES

Furthermore, the units are broken down from a division, to a sub-division, to a group to five hundred and six (506) specific class codes, within an over 500-page book that helps determine where your business is coded (1292.0 - *Australian and New Zealand Standard Industrial Classification* (ANZSIC), 2006 (Revision 1.0)).

When reviewing the divisions, for example Division Q, The Health Care and Social Assistance Division, it includes units mainly engaged in providing human health care and social assistance.

The units engaged in providing these services apply common processes, where the labour inputs of practitioners with the requisite expertise and qualifications are integral to production or service delivery.

The Health Care and Social Assistance Division contains the following subsections:

  – Subdivision 84 Hospitals

  – Subdivision 85 Medical and Other Health Care Services

  – Subdivision 86 Residential Care Services

o Group 860 Residential Care Services
- Class 8601 Aged Care Residential Services
  - This class consists of units mainly engaged in providing residential aged care combined with either nursing, supervisory or other types of care as required (including medical).

  Primary activities
  - o Accommodation for the aged operation
  - o Aged care hostel operation
  - o Nursing home operation
  - o Residential care for the aged operation
- Subdivision 87 Social Assistance Services

Every division, sub-division and specific class code contains details and explanations that inform you about where your business should be coded. It assigns your specific class code from the state gazette codes, which can be and often are different to the ANZSIC codes.

The codes are important. They ensure that you are comparing apples and apples, that is, your business and one in the same class code.

Each country has a coding system for insurance management, some of which are more complex than others, Australia and the United States seem to have the most complex challenges, as we have state by state insurance means and measures. For example, Australia has six states and two territories, but we have four kinds of insurance: state regulated for some states; non-state regulated or risk states; Comcare for employees who work for the Government; and Seacare for those working at sea. In addition, there is the self-insured option for those who fund their own insurance under rules that differ per state, as well as private insurance for individuals who are working directors.

The table below illustrates the complexity of the system in Australia: there are many options and regimes under which a company must perform its insurance duties.

State/Territory/Definition	Regime
New South Wales	State Based Regulated Insurance
Queensland	State Based Regulated Insurance
Victoria	State Based Regulated Insurance
South Australia	State Based Regulated Insurance
Tasmania	Risk State Insurance
Northern Territory	Risk State Insurance
Western Australia	Risk State Insurance
Australian Capital Territory	Risk State Insurance
Commonwealth Employees	Comcare includes: • Commonwealth Government agencies and statutory authorities (excluding serving members of the Australian Defence Force with injuries sustained after 1 July 2004) • ACT Government • Corporations or authorities who have been granted a license to self-insure, called 'licensees'.
Companies Self Insure	Self Insurers
Individuals Workers/Directors	Individual Insurance Brokers, Queensland State Based Regulated Insurance Option
Seafarers	SeaCare

The United States of America has a different agency and regulator for each of their 50 states and additional territories, districts and minor islands.

Compare this complexity to, say, Germany, Japan, Pakistan, Nigeria or New Zealand, where there is just one insurer.

Relativity – Costs Versus Margins of Business

When assessing your costs of damage, it needs to be relative.

A cost of $500k for a premium for one business may be relatively miniscule for another business.

It's all relative. $500 dollars is the "average price" a high-income earner might spend on a designer t-shirt or designer jeans.

The majority of parents would find a request for those same pair of jeans by a teenager outrageous.

According to the World in Figures by The Economist, in India, an average person earns $3.50 per hour. This means they would earn $140 per week or that it would take 3.6 weeks to earn enough for those jeans.

See the below chart that shows how $500 means different things to different people, let alone to different businesses.

So, when you assess $500k premiums the amount needs to be reviewed in relation to your specific business overheads.

It also must be compared to the state averages shown before, as compared to the revenue and profit margins of the business.

It is essential that you share these amounts with your non-financial professionals so that they can understand the significance of the business Damage Costs.

The exact amount is required. Just throwing around numbers like, "It's about 10%..." does not accurately reflect your costs of safety or damage.

Every business is different. It's crucial that the relative amounts compared to the rest of the business costs are understood.

28 APRIL

ILO - WORLD DAY FOR SAFETY AND HEALTH AT WORK

2.8 MILLION
PER YEAR DIE AT WORK

374 MILLION
WORKPLACE INJURIES

$3.45 TRILLION
COST OF WORKPLACE INJURY/ILLNESS WORLDWIDE

3.94%
GLOBAL GROSS DOMESTIC PRODUCT EACH YEAR

Source of Data: Information sourced from International Labour Organisation July 2018

$3.45 trillion is a gigantic number, but how gigantic? We know that there are millions, then billions, then trillions. For most people, to understand how big 3.45 trillion is, they need to understand how this number relates to other measures. Reviewing the nominal Gross Domestic Product (GDP) of nations (as shown over the page) can help us understand such massive values. For example, 3.45 trillion is more than twice the GDP of Canada, according to the Economist. GDP represents the total dollar value of all goods and services produced over a specific time period, often referred to as the size of the economy.

In Australia, the cost of workplace injury and illness in 2014-15FY was valued at A$61 billion.

At Manage Damage, we don't have revenue of $61 million or $6.1 million yet, so $61 billion seems like a huge amount of money.

"Huge" to us, though, may not be "huge" for your business. So keep relativity in mind and be aware of the size of your business and those around you.

Nominal GDP $USA Trillion - 2016

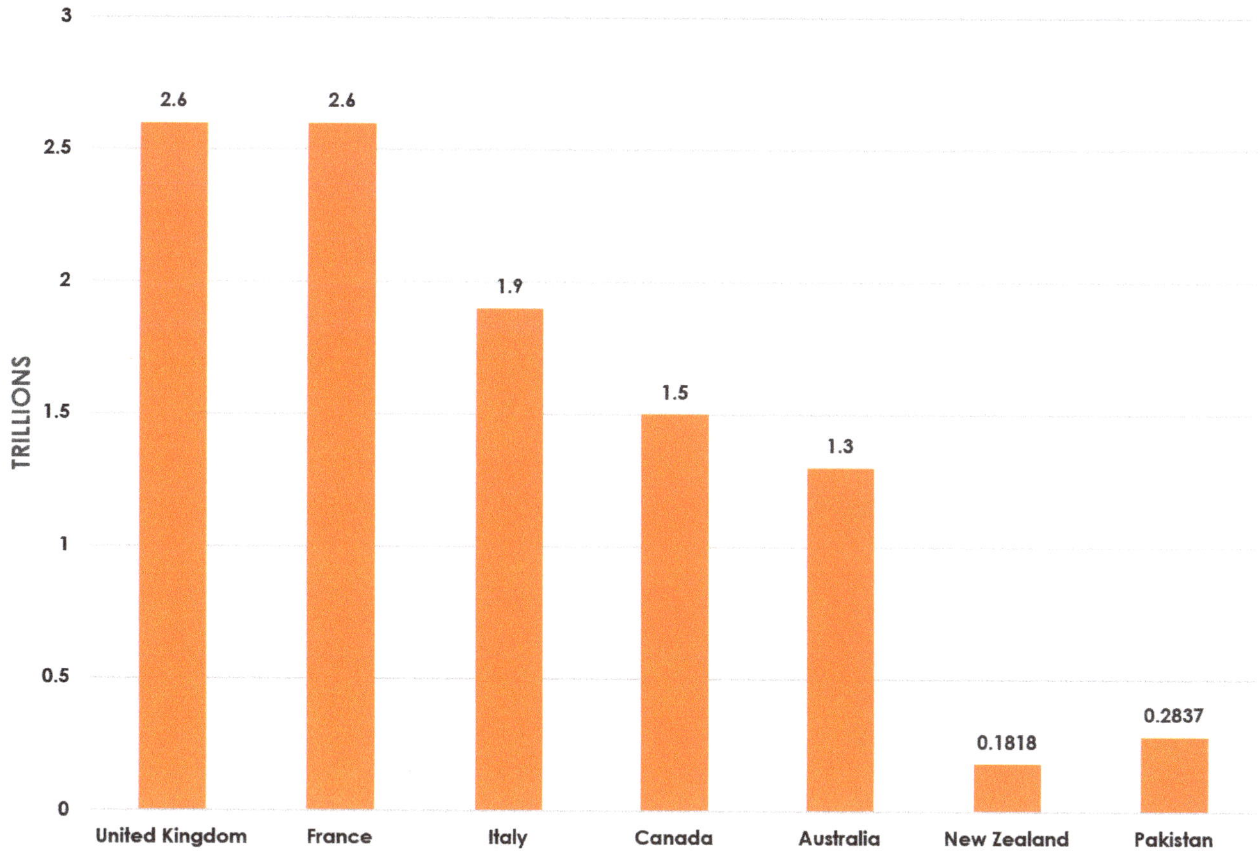

3
2.5
2
1.5
1
0.5
0
TRILLIONS
2.6
2.6
1.9
1.5
1.3
0.1818
0.2837
United Kingdom
France
Italy
Canada
Australia
New Zealand
Pakistan

Cost of Work Related Injury & Disease in Australia Compared with the 2019 Federal Budget Expenditure ($Billions)

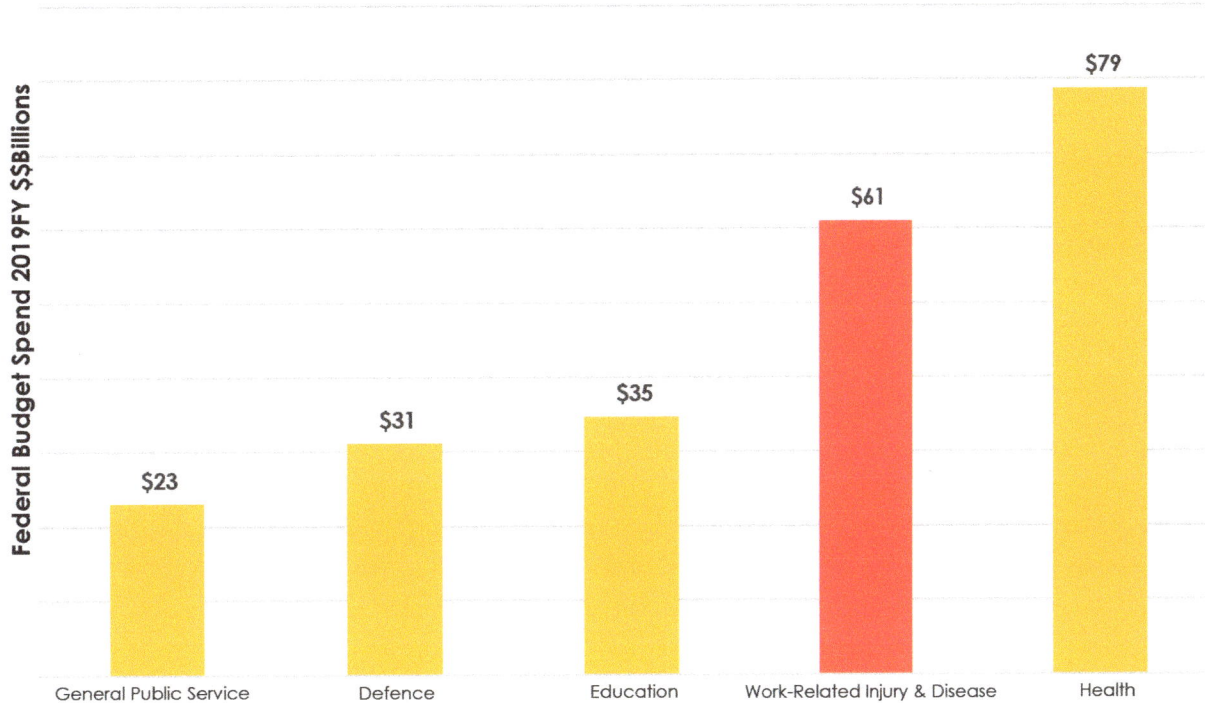

Bar chart comparing Federal Budget Spend 2019FY ($Billions):
- General Public Service: $23
- Defence: $31
- Education: $35
- Work-Related Injury & Disease: $61
- Health: $79

Y-axis: Federal Budget Spend 2019FY $$Billions

MANAGE DAMAGE

2012-13FY Public Data Safe Work Australia

Take this data shared by Safe Work Australia from its 2012-13FY figures: the cost of workplace injury and illness in Australia was $61B. To understand the magnitude of this, we need to make it relative.

$61B is almost as much as the combined projected expenditure on Education and Defence in the Australian Federal Budget for the 2018/19 financial year.

Relative pricing will enable you to make comparisons with your specific industry and therefore calculate your collective risk and group performance accurately.

For example, agriculture, forestry & fishing attract the highest premiums, as they are collectively the highest risk or costs to insure.

The graphic below illustrates the Australian Divisional Insurance Average Pricing from 2011/12FY to 2015/16FY. Use this table to check how your industry relates to others.

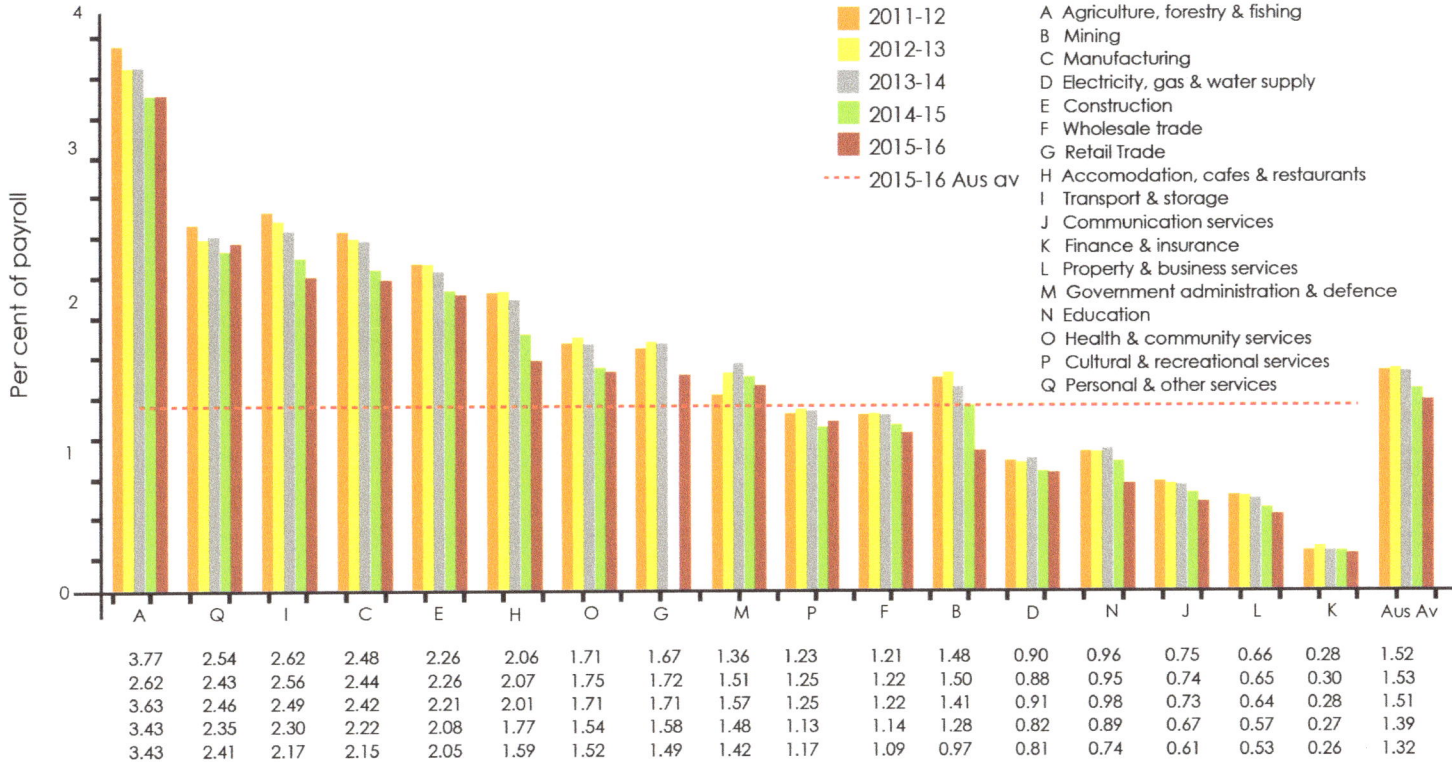

Per cent of payroll

Legend:
- 2011-12
- 2012-13
- 2013-14
- 2014-15
- 2015-16
- 2015-16 Aus av

A Agriculture, forestry & fishing
B Mining
C Manufacturing
D Electricity, gas & water supply
E Construction
F Wholesale trade
G Retail Trade
H Accomodation, cafes & restaurants
I Transport & storage
J Communication services
K Finance & insurance
L Property & business services
M Government administration & defence
N Education
O Health & community services
P Cultural & recreational services
Q Personal & other services

	A	Q	I	C	E	H	O	G	M	P	F	B	D	N	J	L	K	Aus Av
2011-12	3.77	2.54	2.62	2.48	2.26	2.06	1.71	1.67	1.36	1.23	1.21	1.48	0.90	0.96	0.75	0.66	0.28	1.52
2012-13	2.62	2.43	2.56	2.44	2.26	2.07	1.75	1.72	1.51	1.25	1.22	1.50	0.88	0.95	0.74	0.65	0.30	1.53
2013-14	3.63	2.46	2.49	2.42	2.21	2.01	1.71	1.71	1.57	1.25	1.22	1.41	0.91	0.98	0.73	0.64	0.28	1.51
2014-15	3.43	2.35	2.30	2.22	2.08	1.77	1.54	1.58	1.48	1.13	1.14	1.28	0.82	0.89	0.67	0.57	0.27	1.39
2015-16	3.43	2.41	2.17	2.15	2.05	1.59	1.52	1.49	1.42	1.17	1.09	0.97	0.81	0.74	0.61	0.53	0.26	1.32

Reference: Safe Work Australia May 2018 Comparative Performance Monitoring Report 19th Edition Part 3 – Premium, entitlements and scheme performance.
(this report) contains information on premium rates, entitlements and scheme performance of all jurisdictions during a five year period between 2011–12 and 2015–16.

You can further understand this in regards to your specific classification. Beef Farmers, for example, are paying one of the highest premiums in Australia. This cost is also relatively very expensive when compared to the Average Premium Rate per state.

The information displayed in the table explains that Beef Industry Farmers in Australia pay on average 392% higher workers compensation premiums than the average of all of Australia's workers compensation premiums.

Jurisdiction	Average Premium Rate (15/16) Note: adjusted for employer excess and journey claims	Premium Rate Beef Farming (17/18)
NSW	1.34	7.3
VIC	1.31	4.6
QLD	1.19	6.6
WA	1.16	8.4
SA	1.89	5.1
TAS	1.55	6.1
NT	1.62	5.0
ACT	1.74	9.0
Australia	1.32	6.5
$500k Wages	$6,600	$32,500

Understanding your Damage Costs is essential to a successful operation. Once you can make an account of your current costs, you can plan for an improved future: for safety and for your profits.

If you are paying a higher price for your premium, it means that you have been deemed higher risk and will cost an insurer more to insure than another business.

Understanding your risk profile will assist you to make some strategic moves in your business to reduce this profile and, therefore, the cost of your premium.

Damage Costs are Unnecessary Profit Losses

Costs can be Accounted for Specifically

Thousands/Millions Unaccounted for in the Past

Gazettes Public Available Data

Your Business Should Perform Below Industry Rates

Your Cost of Injury & Incidents are Available Now

Relativity - Compare Your Costs

Relativity - Compare Your Costs Versus Your Margins

CHAPTER 6
LOSING CONTROL OF YOUR BUDGET

"A budget is telling your money where to go instead of wondering where it went."

DAVE RAMSEY

Unexplained Premium Costs

Uncontrolled Damage Costs are those connected to a continual increase in the cost of the workers compensation premium and safety related costs.

If your workers compensation premium rose from one year to the next it would be reasonable for the accountant to ask why this has occurred.

However, often businesses are not aware as to why their premiums have risen.

Wouldn't it be nice to know exactly why your premiums have risen?

The cold hard facts are that your premium has risen due to an increase in your risk profile. When the premium has been generated by your insurer, greater risk has been detected, and the premium now reflects this perceived greater risk.

A rising premium could also be due to a changed premium calculation process, which leads to the insurer charging more for the same service; they have increased their profit. This sometimes happens when an insurer needs to increase the pool of money it receives each year from premiums, often due to the costs of insurance being higher than they had anticipated.

Business owners are commonly told that their premium increase is due to industry increases or due to poor performance of the Safety and Return to Work team. However, the actual reason for the higher premiums is always contained in your premium notice, your premium experience ratings or the claims your business is making on the premium. This information is delivered to you at the end of the financial year: these are the facts of the cost that your business has incurred to the insurance company.

The key fact is that you would not be asked to pay this premium amount unless a person was injured at your workplace. If they were not injured, they would not have been a cost to the insurer. The incident would not have made it to your premium data if they had not been injured or received treatment for an injury whilst working for your business.

Your workers premium costs can therefore be summarised as follows: Your premium is a direct impact of your business harm. The incidents that make it to claims are like red flags for errors in your safety practices and business system. When a claim occurs, it's your job to find out where the error that caused the incident occurred and create an efficient solution to stop another claim or accident.

All Business Costs Must be Trended and Accounted For

We know that all risks in a business must be trended and accounted for.

This includes Non-Financial Risks, as we know that this is the best measure of safety:

- These costs are true costs incurred to a business
- These costs are not without a price or expenditure
- They are real dollar values

From a business view, we often struggle to understand how other reporting measures can be used in this area, as they are not relative to any other parts of a business.

Unexplained Premium Increases Limited Our Planned Expenditure

As a business leader, you should not be subject to unexplained premium increases.

These costs do not just arrive the day before 1 July of the new financial year (or 1 January).

Your Damage Costs are occurring all year round and can be regularly reviewed just like any other business cost.

Your end of year and projected premium cost for the next year is a function of your business performance.

If your business is not informing you of an encroaching premium bill that is going to be increased from last year, it's simple: *"your business is not keeping you informed appropriately"*.

The only costs that are out of control are the ones you do not manage; unexplained premium and Damage Costs need attention from your team.

All Costs Must Be Reflected in Budget Planning and Assignment

All businesses create an annual budget and plan for its costs throughout the year.

These costs are then reviewed as the year plays out, measuring their performance against the budget. However, usually the Damage Costs are not reviewed.

Premium Increases can be Financially Debilitating

In some cases, premium increases can lead to reduced margins, to no margin or to negative results.

An example of premium increases occurring on a very simplistic scale is shown below:

Wages: Average $60,000 per worker per annum
Workers: 500 people
Total Wages: 30 million
Average Insurance Rate: 2%

Insurance Scenario	Average Industry Rate Performer	Optimal Performer 90% Discount	Worst Performer (capped 2 x)
Premium Amount	$600k	$60k	$1.2M
Sales/Revenue	$10M	$10M	$10M
Margin (10%)	$1M	$1M	$1M
Revenue minus Premium	$400k	$940K	$(200K)

This example is modelled on a real client who had the same outcomes due to a lack of management for their Damage Costs.

With results like this, your business growth planning and expansion pipelines could be jeopardised as your profit from the year has been shrunk by encroaching Damage Costs.

Regain Control of Your Budget

We've found that, when we show business leaders where their unexpected or unnecessary costs are, they work very hard to reduce these costs immediately.

Knowledge of the costs is the power to assign efforts to its management in a strategic manner.

When leaders know the costs, they can schedule and plan the desired improvements and regain control of their budget.

Need Quantitative Reports from Safety Teams

Leaders require quantitative reports from the safety teams, however the current state of safety reporting is:

- Qualitative
- Subjective
- Scored on scales that are not relative to other factors in business

- Issued without any dollars
- Using counts or single units
- Descriptive

Leaders need to demand reporting that is:

- Quantitative
- Actual
- Factual
- Numerical
- Costed
- Relative to the business internally
- Relative to the business externally
- Trended
- Forecasted

Safe Work Australia recommends that businesses report safety in a financial method. There are yet to be industry-specific recommendations but, with the Risk Dollarisation® method, you can easily frame and create business-specific financial reporting for yourself, your board and your clients.

Costs Of Damage Are Unsustainable

We know that Damage Costs in a business are unsustainable.

A business cannot sustain increases in Damage Costs that are greater than its revenue and profits.

In the example below, the business that is the worst performing is hurting so many people that the insurer has increased their premium to the highest amount. This has created a business's cost so great that they can no longer operate in their current form.

Insurance Scenario	Average Industry Rate Performer	Optimal Performer 90% Discount	Worst Performer (capped 2 x)
Premium Amount	$600	$60k	$1.2M
Sales/Revenue	$10M	$10M	$10M
Margin (10%)	$1M	$1M	$1M
Revenue minus Premium	$400k	$940K	$(200K)

At all times, a business must remain profitable and viable to continue to operate.

Damage Costs can greatly impact a business bottom-line and must be closely monitored for overall business success.

In the coming pages, we will present a number of case studies on this issue.

The first case study is about a Manage Damage client who has a large number of young workers.

According to the International Labour Organisation, there are 541 million young workers (15-24 years old) globally. They account for more than 15 per cent of the world's labour force and suffer up to a 40 per cent higher rate of non-fatal occupational injuries than adult workers older than 25. They include 37 million 15-17 year olds in hazardous child labour.

Many factors can increase youth vulnerability to OSH risks, such as their physical and psychological stage of development, lack of work experience and lack of training, limited awareness of work-related hazards and a lack of bargaining power that can lead young workers to accept dangerous tasks or jobs with poor working conditions.

The second case study is about information Technology, Engineering & Finance workers who face a different set of risks.

These workers are assigned to the Professional and Administrative Services industry, which includes areas of business such as:

- professional, scientific and technical services, including architectural, engineering, legal, accounting, advertising, market research and statistical services, management and consulting, and veterinary services

- computer system design and related services

- administrative services, such as employment services, travel agency and tour arrangement services

- finance

- insurance and superannuation funds

- auxiliary finance and insurance services

- public administration

The majority of these workers are sedentary and office-based, so the highest injuries are found in sprains, strain, musculoskeletal disease and workplace stressors.

The third case study is for Manufacturing, often manual, work with the highest injuries rates found in sprains, strain and musculoskeletal disease.

Manufacturing includes people engaged in the physical or chemical transformation of materials, substances or components into new products (except agriculture and construction). The materials, substances or components transformed are raw materials. People that transform materials, substances or components into new products by hand are also included. Assembly of the component parts of manufactured products, either self-produced or purchased from other units, is also considered

Manufacturing. Such workers often work in plants, factories or mills and use power-driven machines and other materials-handling equipment.

The fourth case is about Construction work, which is any work carried out in connection with the construction, alteration, conversion, fitting-out, commissioning, renovation, repair, maintenance, refurbishment, demolition, decommissioning or dismantling of a structure.

The definition of construction work is broad and includes:

- any installation or testing carried out in connection with an activity mentioned above
- the removal from the workplace of any product or waste resulting from demolition
- the prefabrication or testing of elements, at a place specifically established for the construction work, for use in construction work
- the assembly of prefabricated elements to form a structure, or the disassembly of prefabricated elements forming part of a structure
- the installation, testing or maintenance of an essential service in relation to a structure
- any work connected with an excavation
- any work connected with any preparatory work or site preparation (including landscaping as part of site preparation) carried out in connection with an activity mentioned above
- any activity mentioned above that is carried out on, under or near water, including work on buoys and obstructions to navigation

YOUNG WORKERS - CASE STUDY

MANAGE DAMAGE

MANAGE DAMAGE APPROACH

OBJECTIVE
Manage Damage identified opportunities:

- Savings to the business' bottom line.
- Locating the root cause of the increasing insurance premium.
- Reduction of costs for management of damage risk.
- Enhancing business sustainability for future years' premiums.

APPROACH
Manage Damage views all businesses on a holistic approach. This is a due diligence review that drive insurance premium and damage cost relief.

RESULTS
- Identified opportunities to improve business' bottom line.
- Optimised damage risk insurance pricing and structure.
- Reduced costs to business in relation to current and future damage risk exposure.

KEY ACTIONS SPECIFIC TO CLIENT

- The Client was recommended to undertake a **Damage Costs Sanity Check** by a Trusted Business Advisor - the initial check of their damage risk portfolio and insurance was as a low risk opportunity, to receive expert guidance and identify the potential opportunity for savings.

- Facilitated the successful **recoveries of Workers Compensation insurance premiums.**

- **Adjusted the WorkCover Insurance Classifications (WIC)** for whole of business.

- Provided advisory assistance in relation to new legislation regulation obligations, merger and acquisition activities and **interpreting the legislative insurance premium guidance.**

- Supported and facilitated the business to challenge the Workers Compensation law in relation the retrospective assessment of premiums, specifically challenging a 5 year return instead of a 3 year return.

JOURNEY TO FURTHER IMPROVEMENT

The Client will be implementing the **MetricDriver Program** post current Merger and Acquisition activities which ensure they move to a sustainability model for managing their damage risk portfolio.

KEY LEARNINGS FOR CLIENT

Understanding that the Workers Compensation insurance premium is a cost the business can reduce by improving their performance and their understanding of the legislative insurance premium requirements.

Ensuring the Return to Work processes provide direction that supports the effective management of workers and Workers Compensation claims will provide sustained savings for the business.

YOUNG WORKERS - CASE STUDY

MANAGE DAMAGE

BUSINESS SUCCESSES

Increased Revenue
- $48K immediate saving for Financial Year
- $910K recovery received for over payment of Workers Compensation insurance premiums (returned cash).

Reduced Business Costs
- Reduced Worker Compensation premium insurance costs
- Reduce Return to Work costs.

Reduced Damage Risk Exposure
- Installation of new System and Process Improvements from Review.

Sustainable Knowledge
- Improved navigation of insurance premiums.

Total Savings 2017-22 (est.)
A$244K ongoing benefit = $48K/year
A$1.54M total recovery benefit.

CLIENT BUSINESS PROFILE

Business Activity
- Australia's largest commercial employer of apprentices and trainees
Provides workforce management support.

Business Size
- Wages $40M / Annually
- Australian – across Queensland – Regional, remote and city based
- Majority of Workers are considered vulnerable (young workers) working in high risk environments
- Over 20,000 workers employed in career enhanced roles.
- Managed workers in over 8000 Queensland businesses.

Industry Sector
- Workers across all industry sectors.

BUSINESS CHALLENGES

- Significant Increases in Worker Compensation Insurance Premiums
- This Premium was 250% greater than the gazetted industry
- Majority of business portfolio with Low Experience Young Workers in High Risk Industries
- Construction and Manufacturing
- Limited understanding of the complex and opaque Worker Compensation insurance process
- Navigating the insurance regulatory requirements (specifically WorkCover Insurance Classifications (WIC) Codes Management)
- Less than effective return

MANUFACTURING/LOGISTICS - CASE STUDY

MANAGE DAMAGE

MANAGE DAMAGE APPROACH

OBJECTIVE
Manage Damage identified opportunities:
- Savings to the business' bottom line.
- Locating the root cause of the increasing insurance premium.
- Reduction of costs for management of damage risk.
- Enhancing business sustainability for future years' premiums.

APPROACH
Manage Damage views all businesses on a holistic approach. This is a due diligence review that drive insurance premium and damage cost relief.

RESULTS
- Identified opportunities to improve business' bottom line.
- Optimised damage risk insurance pricing and structure.
- Reduced costs to business in relation to current and future damage risk exposure.

KEY ACTIONS SPECIFIC TO CLIENT

- The Client approached Manage Damage to undertake a Damage Costs Sanity Check - the initial free check of their damage risk portfolio & insurance was as a low risk opportunity, to receive expert guidance & identify the potential opportunity for savings.

- Most experienced agent was assigned due to urgent time constraints for requesting Insurer assess premiums.

- Reviewed current insurance structure, broker & insurer relationships in the Business Group and Damage Risk Portfolio (worked with business's CFO and CEO, as well as managers with in the Group Corporation)

- Installed a temporary Return to Work Agent into the business to help manage the cases, as the associated costs were very high and open worker compensation claims large.

JOURNEY TO FURTHER IMPROVEMENT

The Client commenced the MetricDriver Program immediately to ensure they move to a sustainability model for managing their damage risk portfolio.

KEY LEARNINGS FOR CLIENT

Learning that the true value of an effective Return to Work and Safety/Prevention Team in the business, as there is a direct impact on revenue.

Understanding the best way to manage Worker Compensation insurance costs means a small investment by the Insured Employer instead of incurring all costs by Insurer - this resulted in a significant premium cost increase.

Understanding that the Workers Compensation insurance premium is a cost the business can reduce by improving their performance & their understanding of the legislative insurance premium requirements.

MANUFACTURING/LOGISTICS - CASE STUDY

MANAGE DAMAGE

BUSINESS SUCCESSES

Reduced Damage Risk Exposure
- Installation of new System and Process Improvements from Review Findings specifically around RTW Management

Financial Systems Improvement
- Improved navigation of insurance premiums, systems & opportunities

Increased Service by Insurers
- The process saw improved Insurer response & RTW Management

Reduced Workers Comp. Costs
- Reduced Worker Compensation premium insurance costs
- Reduce Return to Work cost

Senior Leader Engagement
- Enhanced Commitment & Involvement
- New Focus of SLT on Safety

Workforce Engagement
- Elevation and Importance of Safety/RTW
- Improved Skill/Performance Existing Staff

Sustainable Knowledge
- Improved navigation of insurance premiums, systems & opportunities

CLIENT BUSINESS PROFILE

Business Activity
- Workforce Management & Recruitment support

Business Size
- Wages $190M / Annually
- Australian – across all States – Regional, remote and city based
- New Zealand – Regional, remote and city based
- High Legal Risk Exposure = 10,000 pay summaries issued per year on average

Global perspective
- Part of an international listed Group with a M&A growth strategy
- Revenue A$1.563B
- Business Group more than 84,000 workers
- Work across Africa, Asia & Australia

Industry Sector
- Workers across all industry sectors

Major Focus
- Heavy Food Manufacturing
- Agribusiness
- Wholesaling
- Transport & Logistics

BUSINESS CHALLENGES

- Significant Increases in Worker Compensation Insurance Premiums
  - One State Premium was as high as 116% greater than last financial year

- Majority of business portfolio with Low Experience /International Workers in High Risk Industries
  - Heavy Food Manufacturing | Agribusiness | Wholesaling, Transport & Logistics

- Increased costs of damage risk were reducing margins and revenue

- Difficulty navigating Workers Compensation Insurance premiums and processes

- Insurance regulator had formally requested they improve risk management strategies

- Had not clearly identified the problem or causes of problem

- Less than effective Return to Work processes

INFO TECH | ENGINEERING | FINANCE- CASE STUDY

MANAGE DAMAGE

MANAGE DAMAGE APPROACH

OBJECTIVE
Manage Damage identified opportunities:
- Savings to the business' bottom line.
- Locating the root cause of the increasing insurance premium.
- Reduction of costs for management of damage risk.
- Enhancing business sustainability for future years' premiums.

APPROACH
Manage Damage views all businesses on a holistic approach. This is a due diligence review that drive insurance premium and damage cost relief.

RESULTS
- Identified opportunities to improve business' bottom line.
- Optimised damage risk insurance pricing and structure.
- Reduced costs to business in relation to current and future damage risk exposure.

KEY ACTIONS SPECIFIC TO CLIENT

- Business acknowledgement that the Worker Compensation insurance is a scalable variable cost

- Audit & adjust the financial structure so it will support the accrual model for payment of insurance premiums

- Apply immediate changes to Return to Work and employment processes to improve the management of injured/ill workers and reduce the Worker Compensation claims.

- Elevate the focus on Return to Work and Safety risk management across the business

JOURNEY TO FURTHER IMPROVEMENT

Implement recommended strategy for:
- short-term cost savings, which will support the implementation of the strategy activities
- an immediate reduction in risk exposure of the damage risk portfolio
- a pathway to a sustainability model for managing their damage risk portfolio

KEY LEARNINGS FOR CLIENT

Audit & adjust the financial structure so it will support the accrual model for payment of insurance premiums

Learning that the true value of an effective Return to Work and Safety/Prevention Team in the business, as there is a direct impact on revenue.

Understanding the best way to manage Worker Compensation insurance costs means a small investment by the Insured Employer instead of incurring all costs by Insurer - this resulted in a significant premium cost increase.

INFO TECH | ENGINEERING | FINANCE- CASE STUDY

MANAGE DAMAGE

BUSINESS SUCCESSES

Financial Systems Improvement
- Improved navigation of insurance premiums, systems & opportunities

Financial Accrual Improvement
- Ensuring the accrual model for insurance premium payment functions as needed by complex business
- Improved navigation of insurance premiums, systems & opportunities

Increased Service by Insurers
- The process saw improved Insurer response and RTW Management

Reduced Workers Comp. Costs
- Reduced Worker Compensation premium insurance costs
- Reduce Return to Work cost

Senior Leader Engagement
- Enhanced Commitment & Involvement
- New Focus of SLT on Safety

Reduced Damage Risk Exposure
- Installation of new System and Process Improvements from Review Findings specifically around RTW Management

CLIENT BUSINESS PROFILE

Business Activity
- Information Technology, Engineering & Finance

Business Size
- Wages $844.4M / Annually (Aust & NZ)
- Australian & NZ – across All States – Regional, remote & city based
- Around 50% Workers of are white collar & 50% Warehousing/Logistics
- High Legal Risk Exposure = 18,000 Pay Summaries Annually

Global perspective
- Part of an international listed Group with a M&A growth strategy
- Revenue USA$19,654M
- Business Group more than 600,000 workers worldwide

Business Activity
- Workers across all industry sectors

Major Focus
- Information Technology
- Engineering
- Finance
- Transport & Logistics

BUSINESS CHALLENGES

- Significant Increases in Worker Compensation Insurance Premiums
  - One State Premium was as high as 206% more than last FY
- Increased costs of damage risk were reducing margins and revenue
- Difficulty navigating Workers Compensation Insurance processes
- Insurance company audit requested
- Had not clearly identified the problem or causes of problem
- Ran an accrual model for insurance payment of premiums, however the accrual balance was reducing so there was insufficient funds to pay premium
- High workers' compensation claims, costs (which were eroding margins)
- Insufficient Workers Compensation skill available internally (restructured)
- Lost focus on Return to Work and Safety risk management, due to business restructure
- Did not treat the damage risk costs as a true cost to business
- Took for granted that the insurance premium price would not change

CONSTRUCTION - CASE STUDY

MANAGE DAMAGE

MANAGE DAMAGE APPROACH

OBJECTIVE
Manage Damage identified opportunities:
- Savings to the business' bottom line.
- Locating the root cause of the increasing insurance premium.
- Reduction of costs for management of damage risk.
- Enhancing business sustainability for future years' premiums.

APPROACH
Manage Damage views all businesses on a holistic approach. This is a due diligence review that drive insurance premium and damage cost relief.

RESULTS
- Identified opportunities to improve business' bottom line.
- Optimised damage risk insurance pricing and structure.
- Reduced costs to business in relation to current and future damage risk exposure.

KEY ACTIONS SPECIFIC TO CLIENT

- Apply immediate changes to Return to Work & employment processes to improve the management of injured/ill workers & reduce the Worker Compensation claims.

- Business acknowledgement that the Worker Compensation insurance is a scalable variable cost

- Audit & adjust the financial structure so it will support the payment of insurance premiums & forecasting for financial expenditures

- Cost analysis provided new insights into true bottomline in business divisions.

JOURNEY TO FURTHER IMPROVEMENT

The Client completed a successful business sale - the Damage Risk Profile was a key point of difference.

KEY LEARNINGS FOR CLIENT

Learning that the true value of an effective Return to Work & Safety/Prevention Team in the business, as there is a direct impact on revenue.

Understanding the best way to manage Worker Compensation insurance costs means a small investment by the Insured Employer instead of incurring all costs by Insurer - this resulted in a significant premium cost increase.

Understanding the true return on investment (ROI) on Effective Prevention & RTW Programmes

Cultural Improvements from Top Down & Bottom Up for Commitment to Safety.

Financial Incentives for great performance are real & measureable.

CONSTRUCTION - CASE STUDY

MANAGE DAMAGE

BUSINESS SUCCESSES

Improved Business Revenue
- Business rewarded with $16.8M saving (more savings than profit bottomline $11.5M)
- Reducing Workers Compensation claim numbers
- Reducing Workers Compensation insurance premium costs

Financial Systems Improvement
- Improved navigation of insurance premiums, systems & opportunities

Increased Service by Insurers
- The process saw improved Insurer response & RTW Management

Reduced Workers Comp. Costs
- Reduced Worker Compensation premium insurance costs in long term
- Reduce Return to Work cost short term

Senior Leader Engagement
- Enhanced Commitment & Involvement
- New Focus of SLT on Safety

CLIENT BUSINESS PROFILE

Business Activity
- Australian Construction Company

Business Size
- Wages $300.4M / Annually (Aust & NZ)
- Australian – across all States – Regional, remote and city based
- New Zealand – Regional, remote and city based
- High Legal Risk Exposure = many third party engagements

Industry Sector
- Workers in Construction – Residential, Non-Residential & Commercial

BUSINESS CHALLENGES

- Significant Increases in Worker Compensation Insurance Premiums
  - More than two State Premiums were 200% greater than last financial year & well aboveindustry rates
- Significant exposure from active Third-Party claiming on Public Liability Policy
- Increased costs of damage risk were reducing margins & revenue
- Difficulty navigating Workers Compensation Insurance premiums & processes
- Insufficient Workers Compensation skill available internally, due to business restructure
- Lost focus on Return to Work & Safety risk management, due to business restructure
- Did not treat the damage risk costs as a true cost to business
- Took for granted that the insurance premium price would not change

Unexplained Premium Costs

All Business Costs Must be Trended & Accounted For

Unexplained Premium Increases Limited Our Planned

Expenditure & Can be Financially Debilitating

All Costs to be Reflected in Budget Planning & Assignment

Regain Control of Your Budget

Need Quantitative Reports About Safety

Cost of Damage are Unsustainable

CHAPTER 7
MERGING YOUR BUDGETS

"Remind people that profit is the difference between Revenue and Expense. This makes you look smart."

SCOTT ADAMS (Cartoonist)

Time to Merge Your Budgets

At the moment, we see that safety and finance/operations/business leaders are on often on two different pages. Some would say two different books!

Collectively, a typical safety professional and a typical finance professional in a business have distinctly different tendencies or approaches to their work. This is partly because existing hiring position descriptions today call for two quite disparate types of people and approaches.

The two views can be summed up as follows:

Side 1 (Right Brain):   "You can't put a price on safety".

Side 2 (Left Brain):   "You need a price to include in the budget; and less is more".

In many workplaces, generally, the non-financial parts of a business (safety/environment) often align with the right brain and the financial parts (operations and leaders) show more left brain characteristics. It should also be noted that, while people generally have a tendency towards one side or the other, some exhibit both. Plus, of course, some finance/operations/business people show right brain thinking and some safety professionals have left brain tendencies.

LEFT BRAIN	RIGHT BRAIN
Logical	Emotional
Focused on Facts	Focused on Art and Creativity
Realism Predominates	Dreams & Imagination Predominate
Planned and Orderly	Occasional Absentminded
Math and Science Minded	Prefers Fiction
Prefers Non-Fiction	Enjoys creative storytelling

Source: slant.avenua-razorfish.com

You can see the approaches and languages of the two "brains" are polar opposites; hence the opposing views.

Like a kairotic moment, these two "brains" converge when Damage Cost and Risk Dollarisation® is used.

We place safety and finance/operations/business leaders in the same building, room, book, page and line. Neither party wants high Damage Costs. This can be explained via the Happiness Scale for Safety and Operations vs. Damage Costs.

The lower the Damage Costs, the happier the safety and operational people are, as there is less cost due to less harm. Inversely, the higher the Damage Costs, the less satisfaction there is for both parties.

Happiness for Safety & Operations

Damage Costs

This approach ensures that both safety (Non-Financial Risk) and operations (financial risk) want the same outcomes. In turn, this approach helps each understand the other's approach through Risk Dollarisation® and assessment of business Damage Costs.

The benefit is that both "sides", when working together, will achieve the wanted outcome: reduced harm, which equals reduced Damage Costs.

It is important to note here that how people think and therefore communicate is vital to this process. Therefore, you need to think about what language you speak.

What Language do You Speak?

In business, mostly the language of "dollars", "finance" or "numbers" is spoken.

It is often very difficult to understand someone in the business that does not speak in this same language.

Unfortunately, due to theory, systems and processes in the past, the safety (and other non-financial) parts of business have not been required to speak this language of "dollars", "finance" or "numbers".

The new approach of Risk Dollarisation® assists people to understand each other in business. It does this by providing a way for them to meet "at the table" of business to have a conversation.

It is important to acknowledge the different languages in use and acknowledge the need for your system to allow non-financial resources to be bilingual. This will not happen immediately.

It would be fair to say that safety professionals are required to have little to no finance or numbers acumen training or skills. As it has never been requested or required of them and so, when approaching your people to implement this new method, you must consider the up-skilling required for best business outcomes.

You cannot expect a Mandarin speaker to become fluent in Korean overnight, just because you told him to speak Korean. The same is true of the change in language and mindset needed by your safety and other non-financial professionals.

The Risk Dollarisation® approach provides this new language for your business in a way that both sides will understand.

Premium Costs Explained

To be successful in this approach, safety personnel need to understand the premium calculators and Damage Costs.

Finance personnel also need to understand the premium calculators and the Damage Costs.

When both key parts of your business understand these areas, you can influence the outcomes.

How these two types of personnel who hold entirely different perspectives in the company will gain this new knowledge, however, comes down to the language in which they're fluent. Finance personnel already speak the language, so it's a matter of applying it to a new context. Safety personnel, on the other hand, need to become fluent in the lingo before they can get a handle on the application.

Any Costs Variations are Flagged and Addressed

When the Risk Dollarisation® approach is used, safety professionals and finance professionals begin to work together, and you can start to see the trends, balances, deficits and predicted profits. If, like any other budget item, the cost increases, the costs are flagged and reviewed to ascertain reasons for that increase.

Safety and Finance Work Together for Budget Control

When financial and non-financial people work together, you can easily regain control of your budget.

Clarity is regained and factual objective results can be reviewed.

This has a further benefit on the workforce as, in the past, certain "people" workers or staff were assigned responsibility for claims: the injured worker and the safety personnel. The key error points are identified through this process, not at the monthly meeting where Person A's name is read again and again as they are still on a Workers Compensation benefit. Instead, the focus is the costs, when and where that error occurred, and how to avoid it in the future.

Quantitative Reporting from Non-Financial Parts of Business

When this process is in place, Non-Financial Risks can finally be assigned value, and costs and safety can be reported in numbers, dollars and the same language as the rest of the business uses to report their factors.

Safety and finance work together on quantitative results that work toward reduced damages and increased profit. Together, they improve profits and improve safety.

Time to Merge Your Budgets

What Language Do You Speak?

Premium Costs Explained

Any Costs Variations are Flagged & Addressed

Safety & Finance Work Together for Budget Control

Quantitative Reporting from the Non-Financial

CHAPTER 8
VALUE PERCEPTIONS

"There is no truth. There is only perception."

GUSTAVE FLAUBERT

Value Perception

It's important to note the perception or perceived value of anything is subjective.

Left brained people see or perceive value differently to a right brained person.

In Non-Financial Risk in business, the value perception from left brained people has had to be more creative than they would like; they have to believe.

Value is seen in results and the results shown to leaders (lefties) have been in safety terms or values (righties).

The way that left and right buy or want a certain item is based upon two very different approaches, as shown here:

LEFT BRAIN	RIGHT BRAIN
Practical Standpoint	Story Telling Approach
Description of what you get, why you need it and why no other way is quite the same	A short story, mini plot, climax and resolution.
Focus on solution	Focus on outrageous comedy and element of surprise to make the share memorable
Needs testimonials of previous success with same process	Creates a fold out advertisement spread focused on breathtaking imagery and vivid language to captivate the readers' attention
How much they will save on the product if you buy now	Goal is to romanticize the reader into ignoring the competing content of the publication instead of the practicality of the product
What is the Return on Investment?	Sparkling Digital Billboard accentuating luxury or pleasure from the sale

Source: slant.avenua-razorfish.com

Risk Dollarisation® allows non-financial parts of the business to share their great ideas, work and dreams in cold hard factual numbers that are heard and valued by business decision makers.

It is time for our businesses to improve the value perception worldwide. It's time to approach Non-Financial Risk from a financial approach to make people demand safety, safe in the knowledge it makes financial sense too.

User value is normally assigned by either utility, social significance, emotional or spiritual values. When trying to convince a user who is left brain, we need to appeal to the Utility Value Assignment. Ironically, safety is a utility value that also features the economic benefits with high quality and performance… I feel like I'm pitching to the board right now!

Types of User Value (Adaped from Holbrook (1999))

UTILITY
- Convenience
  - Time Management
  - Accessibility
  - Appropriateness
  - Physical Compatibility
  - Avoidance Of Sensory Unpleasantness
- Safety
- Quality & Performance
  - Performance Efficiency
  - Durability & Reliability
- Economy
  - Use Economy
  - Purchase Economy

SOCIAL SIGNIFICANCE
- Social Prestige
  - Face Saving Acts
  - Impression Management
- Identity
  - Role Fulfilling
  - Group Belongingness
  - Maintaining Tradition

EMOTIONAL
- Pleasure
  - Affection
  - Fun
- Sentimentality
  - Memorability

SPIRITUAL
- Goodluck

Moving from Qualitative to Quantitative

To hasten the speed of improved value perception of Non-Financial Risk, safety quantitative and financial reporting is essential.

The past qualitative reporting mechanisms are latent and work negatively to the perception of the value of safety.

These qualitative reports are viewed as subjective and emotional and this again places strain on the value perceptions.

A New Language and Dialogue Between Peers

It's time for a new language. Imagine your safety professional talking to you in numbers.

Finally, you hear them: they are speaking your language and you can finally understand them. They become a peer.

This new communication method takes the form of budgets, Damage Costs and premiums.

Costs of Particular Injuries & Incidents

When costs of damage are assigned, all of a sudden you have a lot in common: you have common language, you want to stop the cost, you want the worker to return to work and you want to find out how you can avoid this in the future.

New Metrics

There are now new metrics within the non-financial parts of your business.

Now your safety people talk about:

- Workers Compensation Rates,
- Insurance Premium Costs
- Insurance Industry Rates
- Average Costs per claim

We begin to acknowledge that, whilst required for tenders, scores like Total Recordable Injury Frequency Rates (TRIFR) are not a value of business.

In the new age, tenders want your actual insurance code rate and they want to know how it compares to industry rate.

It's likely that you currently give it but have no idea if it is good or bad. This could be affecting your tender success rates.

Increase Value Perception

Applying the Risk Dollarisation® method increases value by increasing the value perception of safety.

This approach is unequivocal; your whole business can see the cost and benefits in quantifiable terms ($).

If you don't assign actual dollars, no values are given, and true and relatable measures of improvement cannot be found or shown.

Show Value and Increase Worth, Interest & Focus

When you show the real and true value of risk, it increases the value of safety.

Safety is no longer a belief or a religion; it is a fact.

Business leaders, CEO and CFOs normally just see many costs for safety, in dollars. They are never shown the return on their investments.

The value or ROI is explained in soft non-quantifiable terms, qualitatively or in numbers without meaning; that is, counts or units, not dollars. When dollars are assigned, your safety shares go up, instantly.

Value Perception

Moving from Qualitative to Quantitative

New Language & Dialogue Between Peers

Costs of Particular Injuries & Incidents

New Metrics

Increase Value Perception

Show Value & Increase Worth;

Increase Worth & Increase Focus

CHAPTER 9
RISK DOLLARISATION

"Companies that start by redesigning the economics of an industry often finish by redesigning the whole industry-and owning it."

TIM FERRISS

Non-Financial Risks are Quantified in Financial Terms

For the first time ever, Risk Dollarisation® identifies Non-Financial Risks of businesses in financial or dollar terms.

This approach is a new philosophy or ethos that brings about a change in mind-set.

This brand-new way of thinking means that Non-Financial Risks (meaning a risk to the business that normally is not measured in financial terms) is marked, measured and managed by a financial approach.

By using the approach, real value creation is commenced for the business when Non-Financial Risks can finally be quantified.

Risk Dollarisation® means true understanding of a business risk and its true cost.

Currently, this approach is not a part of typical business operations or systems.

Implementing this financial approach to Non-Financial Risk allows measurement and statistical analysis to replace words and emotive subjective narratives.

Where can Risk Dollarisation® be Applied?

Risk Dollarisation® can be applied to:

- Companies
- Business Units

- Countries
- Employer Self Insurers
- Employer Funded Insurance
- States

The term Non-Financial Risk can be applied to all support/shared services to a business/entity, such as:

- Safety
- Health
- Environment
- Quality
- Industrial Relations
- Human Resources
- Information Technology

Transparent and Accurate Operating Environment

Risk Dollarisation® creates a transparent and accurate operating environment.

The costs of damage cannot be ignored, missed, undervalued or over-valued. Currently, this is not the case in the vast majority of businesses.

The Market Driven Theory Applied to Non-Financial Risk

The market driven theory approach to Non-Financial Risk is one that has never been applied before. Companies have seldom even quantified it, which does make this approach challenging in its initial stages.

Quantifying Non-Financial Risk with this approach has the potential to improve the decision making process and, ultimately, the outcomes of those decisions, as the decision maker has a more quantified view (versus qualitative).

Deductive reasoning is used to assess data instead of inductive reasoning.

With this approach you, as a Business Leader, become an expert on the safety and Damage Costs in your business. You gain awareness of how you are performing now and as compared to your competitors.

Assignable Cost

When you review costs within a business, you normally assign them to where they originated.

The value of every part of business can be assigned according to their Damage Costs.

Damage Cost cannot be avoided/hidden in unique parts of a business.

Risk Dollarisation® provides real evidence and delivers greater insight to ensure a more effective and efficient decision-making process.

In implementing this approach, your business focus on Damage Costs and safety becomes concise and narrow instead of broad and complex.

When you can assign costs, you can assign responsibility to manage those costs. In safety, this has a power that has not been harnessed in the past within a majority of businesses.

New Language for Non-Financial Risk

Risk Dollarisation® is a new language for Non-Financial Risk.

We create new descriptors, with additional and specific costs/values rather than the current values of safety – TRIFR, LTIFR and other malleable reporting values (non-financial).

The Risk Dollarisation® method increases the importance and understanding of the current non-financial functions of a business. This is because they are now represented in financial terms.

The benefits of this new language are summarised in the following table:

RISK DOLLARISATION® APPROACH	OTHER NON-FINANCIAL APPROACHES
Quantitative	Qualitative
Hard Science	Soft Science
Objective	Subjective
Basis of Knowing – Cause & Effect	Basis of Knowing – Meaning, Context
Single Reality	Multiple Realities - Continually changing with Individual Interpretation.
Dollars	Counts
Budgets & Business Cases	Paragraphs & convincing statements/requests

The New Way to Approach Risk/Damage Costs

The new way to approach risk and Damage Costs tests the current theories and concepts of safety.

This approach allows the leaders of business who think in dollar terms and financials terms every day to know and understand the true cost of Damage Costs.

This approach challenges the concept of assigning costs, people and damage in one conversation.

Currently, businesses only become comfortable talking about the costs of risk when there is a catastrophe and everyone says, "We should never do that again!"

Risk Dollarisation® allows a business to accept that Damage Costs can be identified, assessed and managed at all stages of a business, not just at catastrophic moments.

New Key Performance Indicators

Your business now has access to brand new ways to demonstrate the performance of your people and your different business entities in a clear and transparent manner.

Risk Based Decision Making

When you approach risk in your business with Risk Dollarisation®, the decision making process can be taken on a true risk-based approach. The information is clear and available for review and action.

According to Guthrie, "Risk-based decision making is a process that organizes information about the possibility for one or more unwanted outcomes to occur into a broad, orderly structure that helps decision makers make more informed management choices."

More simply stated, risk-based decision making asks the following questions and uses the answers in the decision-making process:

- What can go wrong?

- How likely are the potential problems to occur?

- How severe might the potential problems be?

- Is the risk of potential problems tolerable?

- What can/should be done to lessen the risk?

When you have financial data to assign to the current forms of risk management, beyond just words and lists of risks, this creates a new position for many business leaders. The financial data clarifies the position of the business, in the kinds of numbers that leaders have been seeking.

With clear financial data on your risks, a business can see and demand accurate business cases for decisions on Non-Financial Risks upon review of financial data.

Fewer People are Harmed and Increase in Profits

This approach leads to reduced Damage Costs. It involves a real focus on Non-Financial Risks and therefore Damage Costs will be marked, measured and managed.

We know that once an item is in your budget, it has a line, it has a focus and it has a responsible party through which the costs can be monitored.

Non-Financial Risks are Quantified in Financial Terms

Where can Risk Dollarisation be Applied?

Transparent & Accurate Operating Environment

Market Driven Theory Applied to Non-Financial Risk

Assignable Costs

New Language for Non-Financial Risk

The New Way to Approach Risk/Damage Costs

Risk Based Decision Making

Less People are Harmed & Increase in Profit

CHAPTER 10
SAFETY FINANCIAL REPORTING

"What gets measured gets managed."

PETER DRUCKER

Why Safety Financial Reporting Matters

As a business leader, we expect reporting on all parts of the business. For too long, we have accepted that safety (and other forms of Non-Financial Risk) don't require financial reporting.

It is strange that it has taken so long for safety financial reporting to be expected.

In March 2017, Safe Work Australia made reference and recommendation to safety financial reporting in their publication Measuring and Reporting on Workplace Health and Safety.

They state that:

> WHS reporting needs to provide relevant, robust and timely information to inform decisions that influence ongoing business performance.
>
> Poor WHS outcomes can have a detrimental impact on individuals and their families, on the financial, interpersonal and reputational health of a business and, potentially, on the wider community.
>
> (The) report explores processes for gathering and communicating the WHS performance information that guides the WHS decisions of an organisation's officers.

A New Compass for Business

Safety financial reporting provides a new way to guide the business that has never been available before.

Relevant, robust and timely financial information informs you as a leader to make decisions in a factual manner.

Safety financial reporting provides clarity, objective, numerical and quantitative results that make sense.

Non-Financial Professionals in HR/HSEQ Experience

When Manage Damage initially meet our customers at the beginning of implementation of Risk Dollarisation®, many safety people often feel they cannot or are not allowed to access financial data.

Businesses already normally trust their safety or Return To Work professionals with people's personal medical details in regards to a workers compensation claim or information about damaging incidents. With clearly defined expectations of your safety professionals, there is no reason why we should not trust them with financial data as well. Then the people who are expected to have an impact on reducing the Damage Costs can actually understand what they are trying to reduce in numbers and dollars.

Your safety professionals will very likely require up-skilling to meet the required financial acumen to understand Damage Costs. They were never hired to undertake anything financial, so you will need to invest in your people to add value to the system.

It is time for your safety people to have full access to your workers compensation premium. Many safety professionals have never been shown it, so have literally no idea that this measure is a direct reflection of the damage in your workplace. It has never been in their remit or scope.

Following on from that lack of access, they are also never consulted about the workers compensation premium. Therefore they may not know where to even start to understand a premium or bill. It's so much more than they have ever seen or needed to understand.

If the safety professionals have never seen the premium, it's most likely they also have not had access to other business costs, such as legal costs associated with a workplace injury, the cost of surveillance, the cost of personal protective equipment, the cost of medicals and so on. Therefore, they will not understand how these costs relate to all other business costs, like the fuel bill, electricity costs, water charges etc.

Workers Compensation Premiums are Confusing to Everyone

Workers compensation premiums are confusing.

To be clear, the premiums are confusing to the safety people, the accounts people, the accountant, the brokers and even the insurers themselves. So your people should not feel alone.

The bigger the company, the more confusing it normally is, as there will be multiple entities, multiple states and multiple countries involved.

Safety financial reporting creates some ease and clarity in your vision.

By adopting the Risk Dollarisation® approach, the finance people will consult the safety people about the workers compensation premium regularly, not just when it has increased dramatically (again).

The process also helps finance and safety professionals understand the premium functions and how it works so they can positively influence the outcomes.

By assisting everyone involved to gain the access and knowledge required, the business will be able to increase profit and its safety culture by reducing damage.

Why Safety Financial Reporting Matters

A New Compass for Business

Non-Financial Professionals Have Restricted Financial & Business Acumen

Workers Insurance Premiums Confuse Everyone

CHAPTER 11

CREATE ACTION

If you always do what you always did, you will always get

what you always got."

ALBERT EINSTEIN

It's Time for New Metrics

In safety, it seems like there hasn't been anything truly new since behavioural-based safety about 10 years ago.

We know that, *if you always do what you always did, you will always get what you always got...*

It's time for new metrics. We are creating data and data mining in every other part of business except safety and other non-financial parts of our business.

These metrics are available today through a review of your business Damage Costs. This can be achieved with Risk Dollarisation®, The Financial Approach to Non-Financial Risk.

When we cost safety and assign a dollar value to different parts of a business, we also assign responsibility.

New Information about Business Performance

With the new information now available for your business, a different view is taken and all your people have unique budget lines for which they are responsible.

This fresh information about different sections will accurately reveal performance levels, ones that are often different to what the old measures used for safety indicated.

Pure Engagement

When financial responsibility is assigned to safety, the new information creates actions.

The action is that now someone is directly responsible for a specific Damage Cost and this cost is now in their budget.

Your operational people are masters in how much it costs per unit to do process X or make item Y; now they are going to know how much their Damage Costs are. They're going to become very passionate about it, very quickly.

Information and data on Damage Costs represents the power to find out and isolate specific errors in processes that create damage. Operational people are amazing problem solvers and now they have a Damage Cost budget line to assist them to find improvements for safety in the system.

The Financial Approach informs the business about the specific, actual high-risk areas of operation and where resources may be required to rectify these errors.

The information Risk Dollarisation® provides cannot be disputed: it is clear and factual, numerical and actionable.

Want to Engage?
#RiskDollarisation

"MONEY SPEAKS SENSE IN A LANGUAGE ALL NATIONS UNDERSTAND."

The New Way to Approach Safety (Non-Financial Risk)

www.managedamage.com

Accountability

The most powerful way of gathering attention on any matter within a business system is to create an accountability element.

The new lines of accountability are clear. They are Damage Costs, but instead of just saying, "You have to improve your safety", the business leader is saying, "You are responsible for reducing your Damage Costs; it is in your budget".

If the line is within a budget, it means that it is also a Key Performance Indicator (KPI).

KPIs are often assigned with benefits to the person responsible. New Damage Costs KPIs mean, all of a sudden, there is a vested financial interest in performance surrounding Damage Costs.

Fewer People are Harmed & Costs are Reduced

With this approach, fewer people are harmed, as business sees the value in finding errors and assigning solutions because they understand their costs of damage.

Overall, the business benefits from fewer errors, costs and premium costs in the longer term.

Improved Culture

The Risk Dollarisation® approach also improves the culture of a business.

The financial people understand the costs and the benefits of Damage Costs within your business and wish to improve them, as they are being measured by budgets for which they are responsible.

Mark, Measure & Manage

With the Risk Dollarisation® approach, safety is finally marked, measured and managed with real, quantitative measures, that people in business understand: dollars.

It's Time for New Metrics

New Information About Business Performance

Pure Engagement

Accountability

Less People are Harmed & Costs are Reduced

Improved Culture

Mark, Measured & Managed Results

CHAPTER 12
FUTURIST THINKING

"Intelligence is the ability to adapt to change."

STEPHEN HAWKING

Changing the Way we Work

As a business leader, you would be abreast of some of the changes to ways we work. In particular, there are two major shifts occurring that will have an effect on Damage Costs and safety in a business;

a. The gig/digital platform/sharing/informal economy
b. Introduction of replacement automation & robotics

It is our view that both of these will have significant cost implications for business Damage Costs management.

Initially, it is expected that approximately 40% of new employees will be working within the gig economy by 2020.

It is known that worker compensation claims are a direct result of a redundancy or even more likely for end of engagement on a casualised work basis.

The gig economy is also known as the sharing economy, crowd-work, app-work, non-standard, self-employment or the informal economy.

This kind of work has emerged over the last few years and has some challenges for the companies, people engaging giggers and also the giggers themselves.

Issues emerge when reviewing insurance coverage and tax contributions from gig parties:

> The term "gig economy" is used to refer to a wide range of different types and models of work. A common feature of many of these is a reliance on intermediary digital platforms or apps to connect self-employed workers with work.

Gig economy companies often operate in industries that have historically relied on self-employed workforces.

New technology, however, enables them to operate on a scale which has substantial implications for the nature of work, the sectors in which they operate and the welfare state.

For example, Uber relies on self-employed drivers using its app to provide taxi services to customers.

Taxi drivers in the UK are usually self-employed.

Uber's employment model is therefore not new; but the number of drivers working on its platform (currently over 40,000) means that it has a substantial opportunity to disrupt and reshape existing working practices in the industry. Reference: United Kingdom Self-Employment and the Gig Economy May 2017

Recently the Self-Employment and the Gig Economy Report (May 2017) was released as a result of an inquiry into this type of work. The reason it has been on the agenda is that the United Kingdom, Australia, Germany, France and many other countries around the world that provide services to the people rely on taxes, pension/superannuation, workers compensation and other contributions to run their nations.

Roads, welfare, pensions, workers compensations, defence, education etc. are all provided for by way of our nation collecting taxes to pay for this. This is known as the "Contributory Principle", "a social contract between individuals and the state" that is central to many countries' welfare systems.

When we remove up to 40% of these tax paying, contributing people as they move into informal or gig economies, governments are going to be receiving less tax and other mandatory contributions from formal employers. Therefore, there is less monies being collected and fewer contributions.

Informal work has its advantages and disadvantages:

- Advantage: Profitability – the past employer can find great advantages in the gig economy, as it normally costs a lot less. Staff are not permanent, so you do not need to pay tax, super, workers insurance, holiday pay, leave entitlements and the rate of charge per hour can be less than that of the hourly rate for internal staff.
- Advantage: Flexibility – a worker can choose what hours they work.
- Advantage: Established infrastructure – a worker can benefit from the established worker online platforms, that someone else has designed, which can gather customers/clients for them.
- Advantage: Flexibility for business – a business does not need to commit to a worker, with zero-hour contract work.
- Disadvantage: Employment rights – gig workers have far fewer employment rights and benefits than full-time staff, including no sick pay, holiday allowances, no workers compensation insurance or company pensions.
- Disadvantage: Workers lack insurance – Gig personnel may not hold Public Liability Coverage or it is not appropriate for your company requirements, they may not hold Professional Indemnity Coverage or it is not appropriate for your company requirements, they may not hold Personal Accident and Sickness or Equivalent Workers Compensation Insurance Coverage or it is not appropriate for your company requirements

- Disadvantage: Security – no security in work planned or booked and no confirmation of how much they will earn and when the project would start and finish.
- Disadvantage: Workers competency and qualifications may not meet your company expectations.

When this situation is coupled with the advance of robotics, we are going to see more and more strain on nations that rely on this form of taxation collection and contributions to pay for social welfare.

In the UK alone, it has been estimated that the impact of the rise of low-paid and informal economy work will be an estimated 4 billion pounds a year or a loss of 75 million pounds a week.

It is estimated that up to 40% of the USA workforce will be included in the gig economy by 2020.

So, if 40% of people lose their secure full time job, it is possible that some of the workforce will attempt to make claims on past injuries that occurred at their last workplace. This is not to say that 40% of people will claim. However, if 40% of people are not as well off as a full time employee, they may require social welfare that they cannot access due to their small incomes from gig work. This may lead to people becoming more desperate and making either false claims on past employers or real claims from an injury that happened at a past workplace simply to gain some financial security.

The insurance companies or agencies will be receiving up to 40% fewer contributions to the insurance pools of money to pay for claims.

They might "manage" this by assigning higher premiums.

The problematic situation with gig workers, ABN workers or informal workers is they normally do not have insurance.

So, whilst a gig worker should seek and arrange insurance options for full coverage in case of an accident, they usually do not seek this cover.

When there is an accident, if they are on a temporary assignment, 99% of claims will still be assigned to your workers compensation premium (the company that assigned them at the time of the temporary engagement).

Yes, that's right. You have no control on how they manage their safety, but you become responsible if it happens at your workplace.

"But they are not my worker!" I hear you say. Unfortunately, when you consult the Gig Worker Determination Guides for almost every state and country of the world, you guessed it: if they have no tools, they're not a contractor; woe is them, you must pay.

What Will This do to Your Premiums?

We ran some simulations of the possible premium impacts of the gig economy on premiums Australia wide, for example. This can be simulated for any nation; the cause and effect is the same.

The simulations below are based upon the average wages and premium rates per state.

Cost increments are shown for a variant of business sizes and each state average rates.

EFFECTS OF GIG ECONOMY ON YOUR BUSINESS WORKERS COMPENSATION PREMIUMS

2016-2017	NSW	VIC	QLD	WA	SA	TAS	NT	ACT
Average Premium rate (% of payroll)	1.397	1.272	1.2	1.525	1.8	2	2.33	2.58
Average Premium rate (% of payroll) w Gig Economy	1.956	1.781	1.680	2.135	2.520	2.800	3.262	3.612
10 Staff Pre Gig	11,176	10,176	9,600	12,200	14,400	16,000	18,640	20,640
10 Staff Post Gig	15,646	14,246	13,440	17,080	20,160	22,400	26,096	28,896
50 Staff Pre Gig	55,880	50,880	48,000	61,000	72,000	80,000	93,200	103,200
50 Staff Post Gig	78,232	71,232	67,200	85,400	100,800	112,000	130,480	144,480
100 Staff Pre Gig	111,760	101,760	96,000	122,000	144,000	160,000	186,400	206,400
100 Staff Post Gig	156,464	142,464	134,400	170,800	201,600	224,000	260,960	288,960
500 Staff Pre Gig	558,800	508,800	480,000	610,000	720,000	800,000	932,000	1,032,000
500 Staff Post Gig	782,320	712,320	672,000	854,000	1,008,000	1,120,000	1,304,800	1,444,800
1,000 Staff Pre Gig	1,117,600	1,017,600	960,000	1,220,000	1,440,000	1,600,000	1,864,000	2,064,000
1,000 Staff Post Gig	1,564,640	1,424,640	1,344,000	1,708,000	2,016,000	2,240,000	2,609,600	2,889,600
5,000 Staff Pre Gig	5,588,000	5,088,000	4,800,000	6,100,000	7,200,000	8,000,000	9,320,000	10,320,000
5,000 Staff Post Gig	7,823,200	7,123,200	6,720,000	8,540,000	10,080,000	11,200,000	13,048,000	14,448,000
10,000 Staff Pre Gig	11,176,000	10,176,000	9,600,000	12,200,000	14,400,000	16,000,000	18,640,000	20,640,000
10,000 Staff Post Gig	15,646,400	14,246,400	13,440,000	17,080,000	20,160,000	22,400,000	26,096,000	28,896,000

The results are significantly more problematic for high-risk industries that are being charged a higher rate today due to their specific risk profile.

The possible cost hikes by the insurance companies increasing your premiums to cover for lost contributions by the gig or informal economy does look quite astounding. It is a problem we believe business will face first before governments experience the same. We know that the insurance companies' stance on informal workers in many nations is making the responsibility fall on the hiring company at the time of the incident, not the platform company. This has cost implications to your premiums and your risk profile should be explored prior to outsourcing of employment.

If outsourcing is undertaken, contracts need to firmly assign requirements for specific workers compensation insurance policies for gig workers, and apply the appropriate coverage for public liability policies and professional indemnity policies that meet your company expectations.

POTENTIAL EFFECTS OF GIG ECONOMY ON YOUR BUSINESS WORKERS COMPENSATION PREMIUMS (HIGHEST PREMIUM RATES)

2017-2018	NSW	VIC	QLD	WA	SA	TAS	NT	ACT
Highest Premium Rate (% of payroll)	10.42	8.007	8.393	8.35	7.555	10	15	14.18
Highest Premium Rate (% of payroll) w Gig Eco	14.588	11.210	11.750	11.690	10.577	14.000	21	19.852
10 Staff Pre Gig	83,360	64,056	67,144	66,800	60,440	80,000	120,000	113,440
10 Staff Post Gig	116,704	89,678	94,002	93,520	84,616	112,000	168,000	158,816
50 Staff Pre Gig	416,800	320,280	335,720	334,000	302,200	400,000	600,000	567,200
50 Staff Post Gig	583,520	448,392	470,008	467,600	423,080	560,000	840,000	794,080
100 Staff Pre Gig	833,600	640,560	671,440	668,000	604,400	800,000	1,200,000	1,134,400
100 Staff Post Gig	1,167,040	896,784	940,016	935,200	846,160	1,120,000	1,680,000	1,588,160
500 Staff Pre Gig	4,168,000	3,202,800	3,357,200	3,340,000	3,022,000	4,000,000	6,000,000	5,672,000
500 Staff Post Gig	5,835,200	4,483,920	4,700,080	4,676,000	4,230,800	5,600,000	8,400,000	7,940,800
1,000 Staff Pre Gig	8,336,000	6,405,600	6,714,400	6,680,000	6,044,000	8,000,000	12,000,000	11,344,000
1,000 Staff Post Gig	11,670,400	8,967,840	9,400,160	9,352,000	8,461,600	11,200,000	16,800,000	15,881,600
5,000 Staff Pre Gig	41,680,000	32,028,000	33,572,000	33,400,000	30,220,000	40,000,000	60,000,000	56,720,000
5,000 Staff Post Gig	58,352,000	44,839,200	47,000,800	46,760,000	42,308,000	56,000,000	84,000,000	79,408,000
10,000 Staff Pre Gig	83,360,000	64,056,000	67,144,000	66,800,000	60,440,000	80,000,000	120,000,000	113,440,000
10,000 Staff Post Gig	116,704,000	89,678,400	94,001,600	93,520,000	84,616,000	112,000,000	168,000,000	158,816,000

The way a worker is classified as a "worker" or an "independent worker/contractor" and whether you as an employer would be responsible for your worker's compensation claim is shown in a recent report released by Data 61, Workplace Safety Futures. Manage Damage has added further analysis to this in order to discuss the likelihood that you would be required to cover the insurance of a gig worker.

The question is, who would be deemed the employer and, therefore, be required to pay for a gig worker? Use the table below to determine the answer.

State	Coverage of independent contractors	Is your Gig Person a "Worker"?
New South Wales	Not unless contractor is a deemed worker pursuant to schedule 1, Workplace Injury Management and Workers Compensation Act 1998.	In Gig Definition = YES a Worker There is a Worker or Contractor Tool http://workerstatus.workcover.nsw.gov.au The tool is designed to help you determine whether a person is a worker, a deemed worker or contractor for workers compensation insurance purposes. Worker: section 4 (1) of the Workplace Injury Management and Workers Compensation Act 1998 (1998 Act). Deemed Worker: https://www.legislation.nsw.gov.au/#/view/act/1998/86/sch1 Under NSW workers compensation legislation, many people working as contractors are deemed workers for workers compensation purposes. In these cases, the employer is treated as a 'principal' and is responsible for declaring remuneration for the purpose of workers compensation. Note: a person's status for tax purposes may not be the same as their status as a worker for workers compensation insurance purposes. For example, a person may be a contractor for tax purposes, but still be a worker for the purposes of workers compensation. You can also apply for a private ruling if you are not sure: http://www.sira.nsw.gov.au/forms/s175c-private-ruling-form
Victoria	Not unless the contractor is a deemed worker pursuant to clause 9 of schedule 1.	In Gig Definition = YES a Worker – unless you have a very firm, detailed contract Who is a Worker Tool https://www.worksafe.vic.gov.au/insurance/types-of-workers Tool https://www.worksafe.vic.gov.au/pages/insurance-and-premiums/-contractors-and-workers/worker-and-contractor-assessment-tool
Queensland	No, unless determined an employee using the ATO Decision Tool.	In Gig Definition = YES a Worker https://www.ato.gov.au/calculators-and-tools/employee-or-contractor/
Western Australia	No, unless employed under contract for service and remunerated in substance for personal manual labour or service.	In Gig Definition = YES a Worker https://www.workcover.wa.gov.au/employers/understand-ing-your-rights-obligations/covering-your-workers/

Definition of a worker
The definition of a 'worker' covers:
- full-time workers on a wage or salary
- part-time, casual and seasonal workers
- workers on commission
- piece workers
- working directors (optional)
- contractors and sub-contractors (in some circumstances)

This definition is broad and can be broken up into two parts: primary and extended.
Primary definition of a 'worker'
This covers any person who works under a contract of service or apprenticeship with you. The contract may be expressed or implied, oral or written. A large part of the workforce is covered under this part of the 'worker' definition, including:
- full-time and part-time workers
- casual workers
- seasonal and piece workers
- workers on salary or wages
- workers supervised and controlled by an employer
- workers who may be fired by an employer
- workers who work for only one employer
- workers with set hours of work.

Extended definition of a 'worker'
This covers any person who works under a contract for service. Many people who work as contractors or sub-contractors may be covered under this part of the definition, and it may cover workers who:
- are paid on piece rates, hourly rates or per job
- work for the employer on a 'one-off' or per job basis
- do not have set hours of work
- work for more than one employer
- work unsupervised
- pay 20 per cent prescribed payments (sub-contractor's tax)
- are covered by an industrial award or agreement.

South Australia	Yes, if covered by definitions in s4: • 'worker' which includes a person by whom work is one under a contract of service (whether or not as an employee). • 'contract of service' which includes if person undertakes prescribed work or work of a prescribed class. See also Regulation 5 and s4(7)	In Gig Definition = YES a Worker A worker (for workers compensation purposes) is a person who is engaged to perform work under a contract of service (as defined by the Return to Work Act 2014 (the Act)). Contract of service represents a relationship formed between an employer and employee but in the context of the Act, the definition of "contract of service" has a much broader application. Self-employed contractors and other persons that meet particular criteria are also 'deemed' workers for the purpose of the Act, including people that work in the following classes of work: • building work • cleaning work • driving a taxi-cab or similar motor vehicle • driving or riding a vehicle (other than a commercial motor vehicle) for fee or reward • performing as an entertainer • performing work as an outworker where that work is governed by an award or industrial agreement that applies to 'outworkers' • work of a minister, priest or other member of a religious order except a minister, priest, pastor, ordained minister, deaconess or lay priest of prescribed religious orders • thoroughbred riding work performed by a licensed jockey.
Tasmania	Persons engaged under a contract for services are not covered unless the contract is for work exceeding $100 that is not incidental to a trade or business regularly carried out by the contractor. A contractor is not covered during any period for which they have personal accident insurance - s4B.	In Gig Definition = YES a Worker If the worker doesn't take out Insurance you need to inform the company who has made the temporary engagement and technically then they would be held accountable. Outworkers are specifically named as excluded
Northern Territory	No, unless determined an employee using the ATO Decision Tool.	In Gig Definition = YES a Worker https://www.ato.gov.au/calculators-and-tools/employee-or-contractor/
Australian Capital Territory	No, if employed under contract for services. However, there are provisions for the coverage of regular contractors.	In Gig Definition = YES a Worker "The simple answer is that they could be a worker, an employer or even both" https://www.accesscanberra.act.gov.au/app/answers/detail/a_id/2989/~/workers-compensation#!tabs-5

C'wealth Comcare	No, compensation only through employment of employees.	Yet to be tested
C'wealth Seacare	No, compensation only through employment of employees.	In Gig Definition = YES a Worker A Seafarer who is employed in any capacity
C'wealth DVA	Only if a 'declared member' — s8.	Not very likely
New Zealand	Yes	Yes

Hirer

Seacare

MANAGE DAMAGE

NORTHERN TERRITORY

QUEENSLAND

Hirer

WESTERN AUSTRALIA

Hirer

C'th DVA
Unlikely

SOUTH AUSTRALIA

Hirer

NEW SOUTH WALES

Hirer

Hirer

Hirer

Australian Government
Comcare
Untested

Hirer

VICTORIA

Hirer

TASMANIA

Hirer (Buyer Beware)

Unlikely Due to Hiring Process

Not Yet Tested

The next area of review for the future of the way we work is regarding the automation of specific industries.

Automation has been highlighted as most likely in the following industries:

- Science
- Healthcare/Hospitals
- Policing/Security
- Farming
- Taxi Drivers
- Insurance Companies
- Financial Analysis
- Public Transport
- Construction
- Banking
- Manufacturing

When the ABS data for 2017/18FY was reviewed for the amount of employment per areas, it was found the impacts would be as per the below.

For Australia, this would represent:

- People without full time employment   669,603
- Total Lost Wages from Premium Pools $53,568,254,551

When you remove $53,568,254,551 from the total premium collection pool, the insurers are going to be relatively short compared to how much they have been collecting.

It is known that worker compensation claims can be a direct result of being replaced by a robot or an automated system.

Whilst there is evidence to suggest that workers compensation claims are associated with economic cycles and that claims tend to increase during an upswing of the economy, and decline with a decrease as per below:

Workplace Health and Safety Queensland (2013, February). Construction Industry Report stated

"Injury rates and the economic cycle – a number of studies have shown that workers' compensation claims rates are associated with economic cycles. Claim rates tend to increase during the upswing due to:

- the more intensive use of labour;
- short cutting of safety procedures and training;
- a higher proportion of less experienced new hires;
- less worker fear of filing compensation claims;
- overuse of machinery, without proper maintenance; and
- the use of outdated or unsafe plant.

- Conversely, claim rates tend to drop during recessions as:
- the less experienced workers are the first to be laid off;
- the least safe plant is taken out of services;
- the pace of work is slower; and
- there is more time available for rest breaks, training and observance of safety rules."

This assessment has always been at a time when the workers could seek work in other manual task areas. I would also say that in the past workers compensation claims data that was reviewed was 2001, at this time there were only 75,000 robots units sold and a robot was around $80k, today we are looking at an average of $20k per Robot and sales in excess of 300,000 robots sold in 2016.

In those periods of time workers compensation claims were also associated with very bad stigmas and personnel would be reluctant to make claims; claiming is now a daily occurrence, it is a right and regular part of work.

Consider this approach:

"Injury rates and the decline of an industry or replacement of personnel via Automation and Robotics

A number of studies have shown that workers' compensation claims rates are associated with economic cycles. Claim rates tend to increase towards the transformation process from Employees to Robotics, Automation and Plant

- there is no other gameful work available for manual task employees;

- unions are called in to help workers with transition; unions explain workers' rights about workers compensations claims (can you blame them, these workers have no other likely form of employment)
- long term employees are performance managed excessively to reduce the requirements for redundancy payouts, which can lead to uncomfortable treatment of workers and rise of psychological claims.
- worker filing compensation claims out of right and duty as they have over a period of time injured their bodies and they have a right to claim;
- injury lawyers make contact with employees directly or through referrals to workers who have lost their jobs – Injury lawyers were not as active when the reports have been written.
- psychological claims were not as freely accepted when the reports have been written.
- Insurance fraud is at an all-time high globally today
- The workers compensation system is a no fault system and is pro-employee/worker, if a worker did at some point harm themselves at work then they are entitled to make a claim and they will if they do not have another form, of employment ahead of them.

The Industry Workers Compensation Gazetted Rates reflect the costs borne by various Australian State Schemes and associated declines in industries; therefore show evidence of this fact.

Similarly to the gig economy scenario, should 669,000 people lose their secure full time job due to automation, it is possible that some of the workforce will attempt to make claims on past injuries that occurred at their last workplace. This is not to say that all of these people will claim, but if 669,000 people are not as well off as a full time employee, they may require social welfare that they cannot access due to being replaced by automation. This may lead people to become desperate and make either false claims on last employers or real claims from an injury that happened at a last workplace simply to gain some financial security.

Australian Employment in High Risk of AI/Robotic Replacement

Manufacturing (19%)	
Banking (18%)	
Construction (10%)	
Public Transport (9%)	
Financial Analysis (9%)	
Insurance Companies (8%)	
Taxi Drivers (7%)	
Farming (6%)	
Policing/Security (5%)	
Healthcare/Hospitals (4%)	
Science (4%)	

MANAGE DAMAGE

When we reviewed the Australian Bureau of Statistics data for the make-up of Australian Worker Engagement in 2017 in each of the areas at high risk of automation, we were able to find the percentage of people working in each of these areas.

As a business leader, AI/Robotic replacement requires time, and planned, consultative change management. However, even with all of these factors, one should really expect some fallout and Damage Cost increments. These would be due to human resource replacement in the area of workers compensation claims to make up for years of work at your workplace where a person may have suffered an incident or a number of ongoing incidents over a period of time that impacted your workers.

Current Approaches to Safety and Risk Management

Robotics and AI Risk Management

As the roles of Artificial Intelligence Technologies continue to expand within the workforce, business/world regulators will need to enact suitable legislation to respond to the expected social and economic impacts.

There are significant current shortfalls in knowledge and experience in Robotics/AI Risk Management for safety.

Currently, there is limited law or written requirements mandated in management of a Humanoid Robot.

Our regulators worldwide are struggling to get a grip on the process of robots having personas.

Today there are many robots in the workforce and an ever-increasing number of humanoid robots.

The price of industrial robots has reduced dramatically; since 1996, robotic costs have reduced from $120k to $20k. When the average salary of a person is around $80k in Australia, you can see how this option may be explored.

There are an estimated 1.8 million industrial robots in work worldwide. As robotics increase in their capabilities, more and more shall be seen in the workplace.

THE NEAR FUTURE IS AUTOMATED

Production is increasing dramatically as robots become cheaper to produce

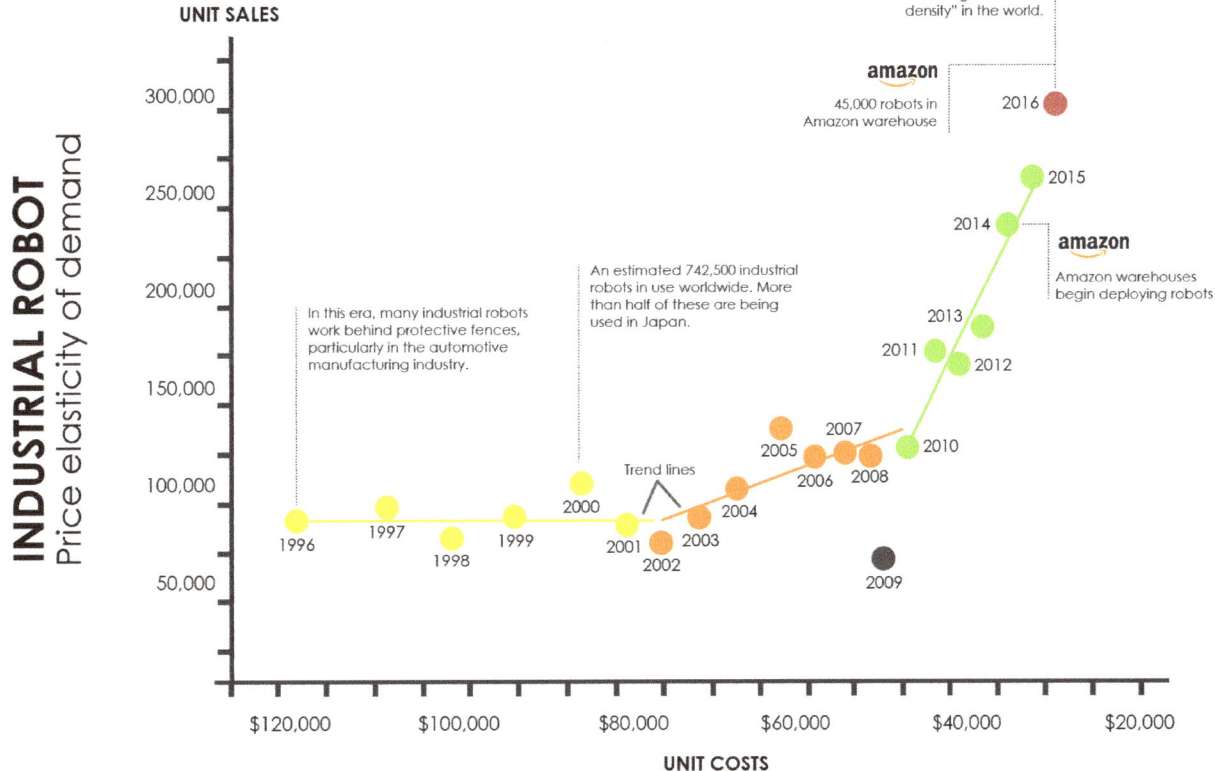

UNIT SALES

INDUSTRIAL ROBOT
Price elasticity of demand

An estimated 1.8 million industrial robots in use worldwide.

South Korea now has the highest "robot density" in the world.

amazon
45,000 robots in Amazon warehouse

2016

In this era, many industrial robots work behind protective fences, particularly in the automotive manufacturing industry.

An estimated 742,500 industrial robots in use worldwide. More than half of these are being used in Japan.

amazon
Amazon warehouses begin deploying robots

Trend lines

300,000

250,000 — 2015

2014

200,000

2013

2011

150,000 — 2012

2007

2005 — 2006 — 2010

100,000 — 2000 — 2004 — 2008

1996 — 1997 — 1999 — 2001 — 2003

1998 — 2002

50,000 — 2009

$120,000 $100,000 $80,000 $60,000 $40,000 $20,000

UNIT COSTS

Source: Ark Investment Management, IRF

Defining Artificial Intelligence/Robotics in the Current Workplace

Artificial Intelligence as it appears in the average workplace today is quite different to what we expect in the future.

Artificial Intelligence is defined as:

"A computer system that can think, learn, and adapt based on user and environmental input"

Or

"A computer system that can perform tasks that humans would require intelligence to do"

In today's workplace, we use AI in many businesses every day.

A recent study conducted by Manage Damage found that the understanding, awareness and risk perception of AI technologies and robotics is somewhat limited. We found that 56.3% of respondents said they did not use AI.

AI can be categorised into two types:

1. Applied AI
2. Generalised AI

Almost every business uses Applied AI daily.

Examples of these include mobile phones, social media, GPS, voice recognition and spam filters.

Without AI, many businesses would grind to a halt! We can surmise that maybe the people surveyed were not clear on the different levels of AI.

When people today think of AI, they tend to think of the Generalised AI – systems that can learn tasks.

ARTIFICIAL INTELLIGENCE (AI)

MANAGE DAMAGE

TYPE 1

APPLIED AI – Systems that can perform specific tasks

Mobile Phones	Social Media	GPS	Financial Analysis	Voice Recognition	Face Detection	Spam Filtering	Targeted Advertisement
Self-Driving Cars	Robots	Monitoring Systems	Automated Machines	Chemical Process	Industrial Defect	Advanced Emergency System	Medical Diagnostics

WHAT IS AI?

Applied AIs use machine learning to learn and adapt without needing to be programmed. On the net, these AIs watch your activity and use it to make new suggestions.

Applied AIs can also be combined with sensors to create machines that can learn from the environment.

TYPE 2

GENERALIZED AI – systems that can learn any task

Google Deepmind	Open AI	Suprintelligent AIs?

Generalized AIs are AIs with human or above intelligence that can perform any task. They do not currently exist, but leading experts believe it may be on the horizon.

Artificial Intelligence is not just a technology of the future - it is here now & is everywhere around us

The future of business is very interesting as we move towards more advanced robotics.

In modern society, we have many robots or robotic plant or systems that can perform specific tasks.

Some of these tasks have replaced human interactions. For example, where a person used to serve us at the checkout, we now have a "self-serve" checkout. Another example of this is fuel station "self-serve" fuel pumps. Some would say this is altering the process from a human-to-human interaction to a machine-to-human interaction, changing the whole system.

With advanced robotic solutions in play, such as the Humanoid Robot, the future becomes even more interesting.

The intended characteristics of Humanoid Robots are very thought provoking:

- self-maintaining
- autonomous learners
- avoid harmful situations to people, property, and itself
- safe interacting with human beings and the environment

The intended purpose of the Humanoid Robot, according to Muhammad Awais and Dominic Henrich is:

to combine the intelligence and situation dependent decision making capabilities of a human with the accuracy and power of a robot.

The outcome of this is that more simplistic and/or dangerous tasks can and will be replaced by Humanoid Robots.

For example, today there is a NAO Robot manning the desks as a receptionist/concierge in the Sydney JLL office. Her name is JiLL.

Originally from France and Japan, JiLL is a 57 cm tall, 5.4kg NAO robot. She joined the JLL team as the firm's corporate front of house administration team for its newest office at 50 Carrington Street, Sydney Australia.

JiLL works as part of a fully automated visitor management solution. JiLL will greet and support staff, visitors and couriers with a range of front of house tasks, including check-in for meetings, providing directions, contacting hosts and recording and reporting technology or building maintenance issues.

JiLL's current duties include:

- Assisting visitors with appointments
- Providing directions to washrooms
- Supporting deliveries and collections
- Assisting with forgotten access passes
- Recording and reporting building related faults
- Recording and reporting IT faults

JiLL is just a single example of the many Automated Processes available today. With Humanoid Robots, the aim is to service humans.

Humanoid robotics is advancing in healthcare/hospitals, policing/security, defence, farming, taxi driving, public transport, construction and manufacturing.

In Jobs Lost, Jobs Gained: Workforce Transitions, McKinsey & Company indicates that, by 2030, work robots could replace as many as 800 million workers worldwide.

Automation will have a far-reaching impact on the global workforce.

Technical automation potential

~50% of current work activities are technically automatable by adapting currently demonstrated technologies

6 of 10 current occupations have more than 30% of activities that are technically automatable

Impact of adoption by 2030

Work potentially displaced by adoption of automation, by adoption scenario, % of workers (FTEs[1])

Slowest	Midpoint	Fastest
0%	**15%**	30%
(10 million)	(400 million)	(800 million)

Workforce that could need to change occupational category, by adoption scenario,[2] % of workers (FTEs)

Slowest	Midpoint	Fastest
0%	**3%**	14%
(<10 million)	(75 million)	(375 million)

Impact of demand for work by 2030 from 7 select trends[3]

Trendline demand scenario, % of workers (FTEs)

Low	Hight
15%	22%
(390 million)	(590 million)

Step-up demand scenario, % of worker (FTEs)

6%	11%
(165 million)	(300 million)

Total, % of workers (FTEs)

21%	33%
(555 million)	(890 million)

In addition, of the 2030 workforce of 2.66 billion, 8-9% will be in new occupations[4]

[1] Full-time equivalents.
[2] In trendline labor-demand scenario.
[3] Rising incomes; healthcare from aging; investment in technology, infrastructure, and buildings; energy transitions; and marketization of unpaid work. Not exhaustive.
[4] See Jeffrey Lin, "Technological adaption, cities, and new work," Review of Economics and Statistics, Volume 93, Number 2, May 2011.

McKinsey&Company | *Source: McKinsey Global Institute analysis*

The optimists would say: "Isn't this great? The robots will replace the high-risk workers and then there will be fewer harm/Damage Costs!"

We take a more conservative view and consider some of the challenges before the opportunities.

In a recent report the prediction for the USA is that:

- Banking and lending could see 1.2 million jobs at risk and a potential $450 billion in savings to the industry,
- Insurance follows, with 865,000 jobs at risk and a projected $400 billion in savings; and
- The investment management sector could face as many as 460,000 jobs at risk, equivalent to as much as $200 billion in savings.

We must note the kinds of tasks being replaced. These are at the entry, middle and technical levels, and range from tasks that can be narrowly defined to those that involve unstructured data sets.

Artificial Intelligence is being applied across Financial Services

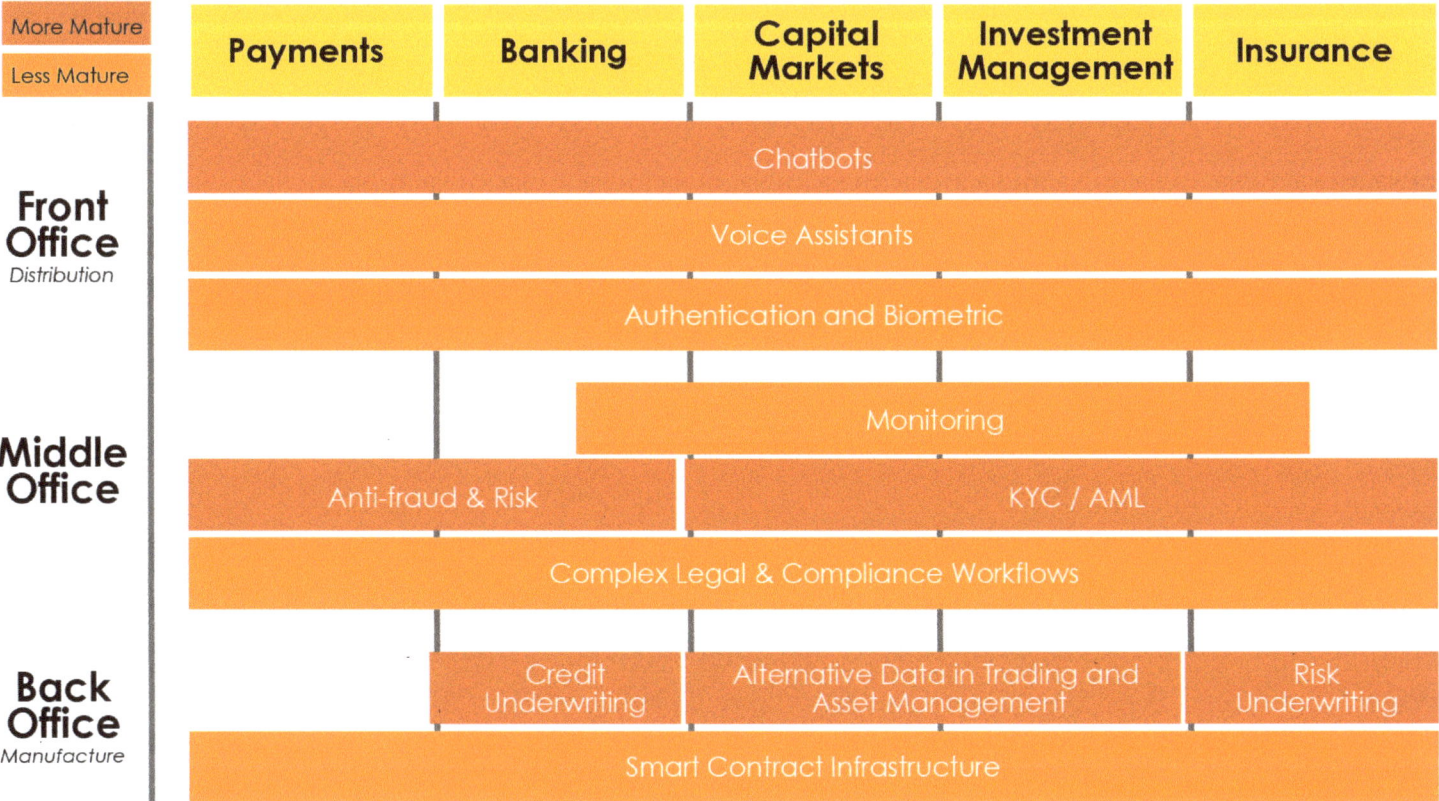

Fintech AI Use-cases				
Payments	Banking	Capital Markets	Investment Management	Insurance

Front Office *Distribution*
- Chatbots
- Voice Assistants
- Authentication and Biometric

Middle Office
- Monitoring
- Anti-fraud & Risk
- KYC / AML
- Complex Legal & Compliance Workflows

Back Office *Manufacture*
- Credit Underwriting
- Alternative Data in Trading and Asset Management
- Risk Underwriting
- Smart Contract Infrastructure

More Mature / Less Mature

Source: Autonomous NEXT

If this is the impact for the USA; a relativity assessment for Australia shows the probability of impacts being:

- Banking and lending could see the 84K jobs at risk and a potential $31.5 billion in savings to the industry;
- Insurance follows, with 60.5K jobs at risk and a projected $28 billion in savings; and
- The Investment management sector could face as many as 32.2K jobs at risk, equivalent to as much as $14 billion in savings.

The replacement is in the simpler tasks and occupations. Therefore, if all the simpler tasks that are less demanding are replaced, what will happen to the people who have become accustomed to performing those tasks?

Scale

Our bottoms up analysis is consistent with other studies about the expected size of the impact from Artificial Intelligence on financial services

Brain sees a potential $5.4 trillion shortfall in GDP by 2030, which would translate to $1.1 trillion of associated GDP in the financial sector

Accenture sees AI adding $1.2 trillion in financial services value by 2035

Productivity Gains from Automation (Bain 2018)

Industry	%
Manufacturing	55%
Accommodation and...	51%
Retail	49%
Mining	46%
Transportation	46%
Utilities	39%
Agriculture	36%
Wholesale trade	34%
Information	32%
Construction	32%
Other	28%
Administrative and ...	27%
Arts & entertainment	27%
Professional services	25%
Finance and insurance	25%
Management	23%
Government	21%
Healthcare	18%
Real estate	16%
Education	10%

AutomationPotential of Industry (McKinsey 2017)

Industry	%
Accommodation and...	73%
Manufacturing	60%
Agriculture	58%
Transportation	57%
Retail trade	53%
Mining	51%
Other services	49%
Construction	47%
Utilities	44%
Wholesale trade	44%
Finance and insurance	43%
Arts & entertainment	41%
Real estate	40%
Administrative	39%
Healthcare	36%
Information	35%
Professionals	35%
Management	35%
Education Services	27%

Source: Autonomous NEXT, Brain 2018, McKinsey 2017, Accenture 2017

Reskilling and retraining for the simpler skillset is a global challenge.

In the past, if someone was replaced by a machine or system, they simply retrained to another (simple) skillset. The challenge here is there will be fewer simplistic roles to undertake globally.

Those who are replaced by robots in any form will suddenly feel every possible work-related ailment they have ever had. It's a chance for a worker to secure some money before they are no longer earning and making a livelihood for their families.

We expect a significant rise in Damage Costs. As discussed before, there will also be a rise in premiums, as there are fewer insurable units/people.

Will they make Humanoid Robots pay tax and be insured? There is a lot of discussion about this, as there will be less insurance and taxes going around to pay for publicly funded items like roads and hospitals.

For those who remain in the new workplace, Humanoid Robots will become our friends.

Humanoid Robots will pick us up and deliver us to work in our electric self-driving cars (with Humanoid Driver).

Then the office doors will open for us and we will be greeted by facial recognition and a robotic receptionist who will ask us about our weekend.

They would have been able to scan your social media pages and will ask you,

"How did you enjoy your friend Katie's Wedding – she looks really lovely. It was at the Gold Coast; I saw the weather was a little chilly. Did you remember to take a jacket? I hope you were not cold".

They will also advise that,

"Your first appointment with Michael should be on-time as the Tesla Humanoid Driver just contacted me and said he would be arriving at 9.06am. Shall I have your presentation ready and I will bring you your coffee order – the same as usual?"

This is just the first 5 minutes of your workday.

Every single staff member will be treated the same, as the Humanoid Robot (hopefully) will have been trained to have zero bias for gender, colour, height, hair type or religion.

I think I would probably like and respect a Humanoid Robot who could be so helpful, not just because I had been busy working a relationship with them over the last 6 months. All persons would receive the same treatment regardless.

These new colleagues will potentially be some of the easiest ones to make "friends" or connections with almost instantly as you join a business.

They will probably also be in your work morning tea breaks or lunchrooms. Staff will demand that they too have a break as they explore the status of Electronic Personhood. They may even have the same rights and opportunities as a usual staff member.

Possible AI/Robotics in Future

It is predicted that, in our future, Humanoid Robots can and will take on all the usual forms of work that we perform today as humans, including:

- Full Time
- Part-Time
- Temporary
- Labour Hire
- Replacement Fill

In all the ways we employ people today, we could be employing a robot in days to come.

Some have even discussed Sole Trader Robots…

Let's take a labour hire example. Your factory processes require an upgrade or annual maintenance regime. Normally, you would hire a Shut Down Crew who would enter your workplace and, under direction, do a number of tasks. These tasks are known, scheduled, listed and planned.

Instead, you could hire a Sparky/Electrician Humanoid, a Maintenance Fitter Humanoid and a Labourer Humanoid, as many as you want. You simply take your tasks or chip of tasks and load them into the Humanoids as they arrive.

The Humanoid Crew is autonomous in how they arrive. They may even pick and pack themselves into the driverless car and have a GPS location given to travel to your factory. When they arrive, they'll meet your Humanoid Receptionist. They might make a cute robot joke (hopefully, not sexually inclined) and then check in. The receptionist inserts their induction chip, which hard codes all the rules and GPS locations of all items. Then she/he asks the Team to report to you, the Maintenance Manager. Then, either you or the receptionist would insert the chip of data about your planned maintenance.

Each Tradie/Robot is specifically skilled in their trade and is programmed to remember all of this training/coding.

You allocate tasks and can manage them onsite or offsite via your monitoring system that can see assigned tasks, times and duties. If a problem arises, you can intercept or they can ask if there is an error in either their code or the environment.

This is a one-off hire. According to CB Insights, there will also be "Robot Babysitters" who will monitor the Robots in your workplace, replacing the job of some of the blue-collar personnel.

Imagine the opportunity with engagement in this advanced state. It's most certainly going to make some changes to the way we work.

If your Humanoid Robot is experiencing errors, they would tell you via their software systems or would return to base after an alert or a failure (like your MavicPro Drone, for example).

However, interesting data shows that, whilst Humanoid and other AI Robotics do have error rates, since 2015 it is lower than the rate of a human, for example, in visual recognition. Of course this is just one measure of accuracy and should be considered as part of a whole view upon design of AI systems and Robotics.

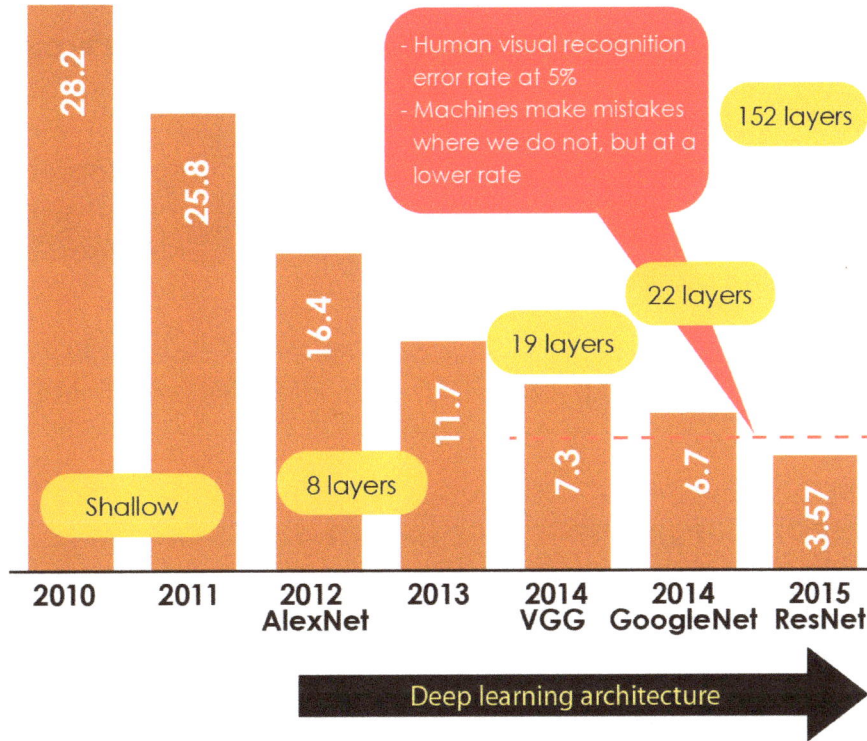

Error Rate in Image Recognition in the ImageNet Competition (%)

It is said that today's current technology in driverless cars, for example, which led to the recent Uber Fatal crash, is not yet "ready"...

> *"No automaker or tech company have current sensor & computer systems advanced enough for production-ready Level 4 or 5 self-driving."*
>
> *"....with the quality & ability of the sensors & the computer processing speed & performance, there is no possibility to have highly autonomous cars without accidents......," Dr Fröhlich insisted (BMW Engineer)*

The impacts of this kind of damage is vast and in dollars. For example, when an incident occurred at the Tesla Fremont factory in California in April 2018, the impact was the company value dropped 2% on the market (to make it relative, 2% of about 50 billion is 1 billion dollars).

A company like Tesla, whilst working in manufacturing, is actually working in quite low risk manufacturing. However, when you are a high-profile business, the greatest impacts for the business are around reputation and stocks. For a radical, new age, emotive-driven buyers company like Telsa, this means great and significant impacts even with incident rates that are lower than competitors. This is because the spotlight is red hot on the Tesla factory due to its prominence.

Changes in the Way we Work Means Changes in Law

There is global discussion about the changes required to legislation about the use of Humanoid Robots and modern machines (plant).

In particular, the Draft European Parliament Committee on Legal Affairs 2015/2103 (INL) released recommendations on Civil Law Rules on Robotics.

This report caused a fury of discussion for and against. Primarily, the discussion was around "Electronic Personhood", a new concept whereby robots would be considered, in some circumstances, as humans.

This probably sounds like a wild revelation to most people, but today there is at least one robot that has been granted citizenship in Saudi Arabi, Sophia. She is living evidence of the concept of "Electronic Personhood" as a reality.

To quote Hanson Robotics directly;

> *Sophia is Hanson Robotics' latest and most advanced robot to date and a cultural icon.*
>
> *She has become a media darling, appearing on major media outlets around the world, igniting the interest of people regardless of age, gender, and culture, even gracing the cover of one of the top fashion magazines.*
>
> *Her press coverage has a potential reach of over ten billion readers in 2017.*
>
> *Sophia is a highly sought-after speaker in business and showed her prowess and great potential across many industries. She has met face-to-face with key decision makers in banking, insurance, auto manufacturing, property development, media, and entertainment.*
>
> *In addition, she has appeared onstage as a panel member and presenter in high-level conferences, covering how robotics and artificial intelligence will become a prevalent part of people's lives.*

Her reputation extends beyond business into the global social arena.

She was named the world's first United Nation Innovation Champion by United Nations Development Program (UNDP) and will have an official role in working with UNDP to promote sustainable development and safeguard human rights and equality.

Sophia is an evolving genius machine. Her incredible human likeness, expressiveness, and remarkable story as an awakening robot over time make her a fascinating front-page technology story.

The legislation in almost every country and every state is yet to catch up with the changes brought about by the development of Humanoids. Their uses simply fly past the regulators and lawmakers.

What we thought was a far off ideal is quickly becoming a reality.

The way law approaches AI/robotics is primarily by appointing it as a plant or a system of work. In reviewing the local Australian law, we made some recommendations about areas in which we think the current approaches will be problematic for law makers and law abiding companies.

In the appendix, we discuss:

 - The Law Reference Section
 - Its Description
 - Possible shortfalls for AI
 - Issues that may be posed

- Recommendations and possible solutions

The guidance material in Codes and Reference Material is also yet to be adjusted to meet the current needs, especially in the space and place of design and safety in design.

Our globalised supply chains mean that we will also be relying on designs and safe designs from other nations globally.

We expect this will be a challenge for our current safety and risk managers. Soon our safety team will be expected to code too!

Risk Assessments will need to be conducted to address the inputs, outputs and risks associated with the design of the robots joining your workplace.

EVOLUTION SAFETY-HUMAN

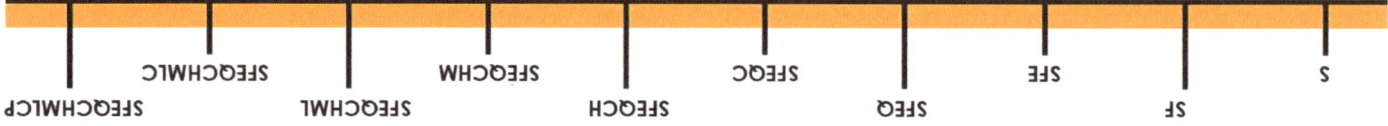

25 m yrs go	1 m yrs go	18 yrs ago	16 yrs ago	9 yrs ago	7 yrs ago	6 yrs ago	2 yrs ago	Present	Next Year
S	SF	SFE	SFEG	SFEGC	SFEGCH	SFEGCHM	SFEGCHML	SFEGCHMLC	SFEGCHMLCP

25 m yrs go	1 m yrs go	18 yrs ago	16 yrs ago	9 yrs ago	7 yrs ago	6 yrs ago	2 yrs ago	Present	Next Year
									PROGRAMMER &
								CYBER &	CYBER &
							LEGAL &	LEGAL &	LEGAL &
						MENTAL HEALTH &	MENTAL HEALTH &	MENTAL HEALTH &	MENTAL HEALTH &
				HEALTH &	HEALTH &	HEALTH &	HEALTH &	HEALTH &	HEALTH &
			CULTURE &	CULTURE &	CULTURE &	CULTURE &	CULTURE &	CULTURE &	CULTURE &
		QUALITY &	QUALITY &	QUALITY &	QUALITY &	QUALITY &	QUALITY &	QUALITY &	QUALITY &
	ENVIRONMENT &	ENVIRONMENT &	ENVIRONMENT &	ENVIRONMENT &	ENVIRONMENT &	ENVIRONMENT &	ENVIRONMENT &	ENVIRONMENT &	ENVIRONMENT &
FIRST AID &	FIRST AID &	FIRST AID &	FIRST AID &	FIRST AID &	FIRST AID &	FIRST AID &	FIRST AID &	FIRST AID &	FIRST AID &
SAFETY	SAFETY	SAFETY	SAFETY	SAFETY	SAFETY	SAFETY	SAFETY	SAFETY	SAFETY

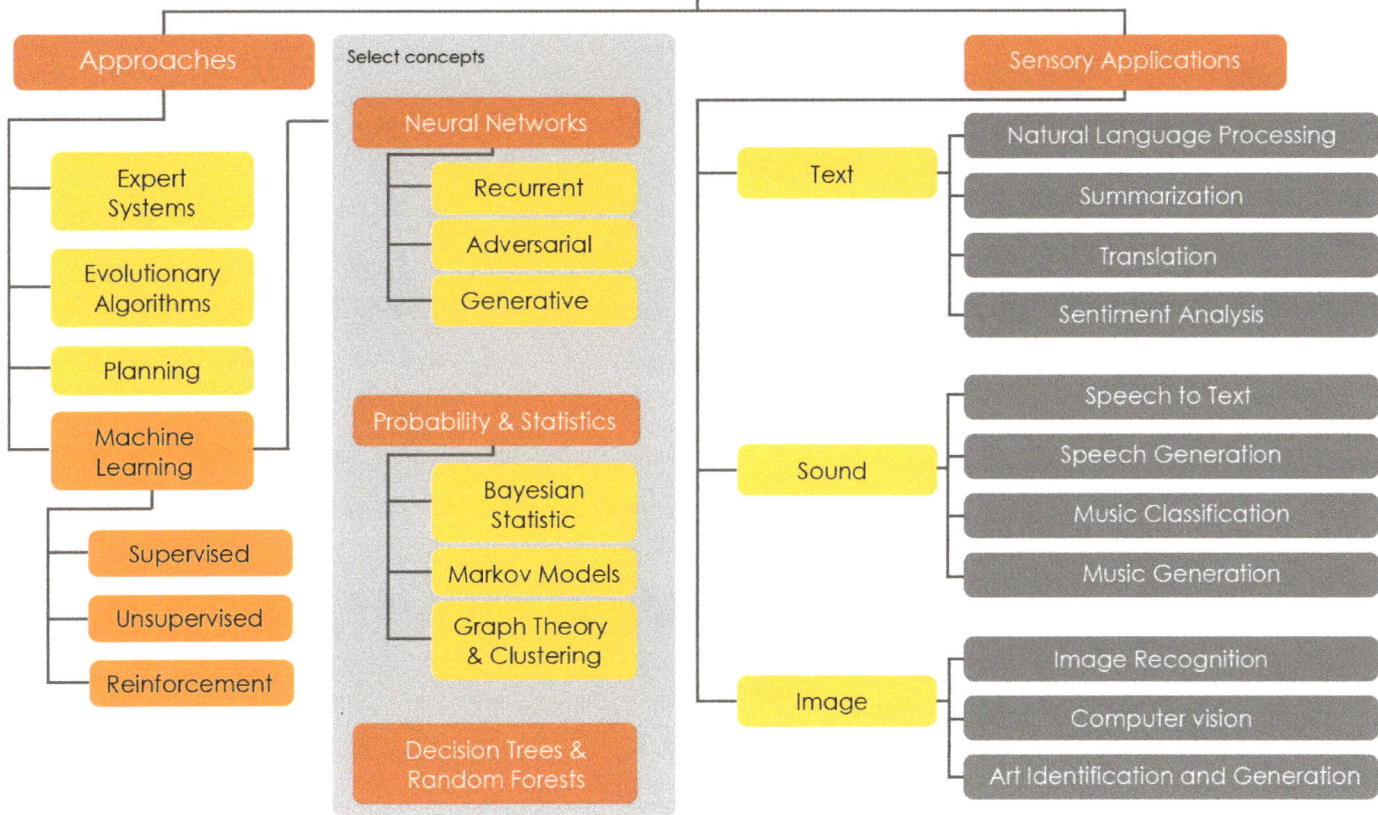

Artificial Intelligence

- **Approaches**
  - Expert Systems
  - Evolutionary Algorithms
  - Planning
  - Machine Learning
    - Supervised
    - Unsupervised
    - Reinforcement

- **Select concepts**
  - Neural Networks
    - Recurrent
    - Adversarial
    - Generative
  - Probability & Statistics
    - Bayesian Statistic
    - Markov Models
    - Graph Theory & Clustering
  - Decision Trees & Random Forests

- **Sensory Applications**
  - Text
    - Natural Language Processing
    - Summarization
    - Translation
    - Sentiment Analysis
  - Sound
    - Speech to Text
    - Speech Generation
    - Music Classification
    - Music Generation
  - Image
    - Image Recognition
    - Computer vision
    - Art Identification and Generation

Sources: Autonomous NEXT, Machine Learning Mastery

It's time for all of us to understand the new age risks with the way we work. To do this, we first must understand how they work.

Above is an excellent display of how Artificial Intelligence works from a design perspective. We think this is an excellent way to commence some of the best review of your risk in AI before it enters your workplace.

As the code is being developed, it must also be aligned with the business rules, regulations and ethics, and designed to fit with your workplace goals.

We expect that, in the future, your local Government Safety Inspectors will be asking:

- Where is your Robot Risk Assessment, please?
- Where are the user manuals for all the users?
- Yes, they are engineers but the law says they need to also produce Safety in Design information.

We have found that, globally, the transition for design considerations for plant is poorly understood and approached. When we start introducing more complex machines, we will need to be better informed.

To make it as straightforward as possible, remember this: your Humanoid Robot is simply the best "plant" money can buy and you must still treat it as a "piece of plant" when installing. However, you'll need to consider its Electronic Personhood too.

As business leaders planning installation of Humanoid Robots, when designing plant (or our robot), we must consider all the phases in the lifecycle of our plant/robot from manufacture through to use, dismantling and disposal.

Our robot must be designed:

- For safe erection & installation (this could make those who work at the humanoid sex toy factory blush).
- To facilitate safe use by considering the interacting people, the maximum number of tasks a robot can be expected to perform at any one time, and the layout of the work area or environment in which the robot/plant may be used.
- With consideration for intended use & reasonably foreseeable misuse.
- With consideration for the difficulties the business may face when maintaining or repairing the plant/robot. Remember, some will be self-maintenance, however some self-maintenance elements must move to external maintenance; that is there will be some tasks the robot can complete themselves for maintenance however some may be more technical and may require external maintenance by other specialist Robot mechanics.
- With consideration of types of failure or malfunction. The plant/robot must be designed to fail in a safe manner and the designers have a lot of input into this element.
- Using a good understanding of the lifecycle of the item, including the needs of users and the environment in which that item may be used.

The law in many developed nations requires Risk Assessments for each and every user.

The law has requirements for:

- The designers of the plant (machines, robots, tools etc. if you make it and people can use it) – "external" characteristics.

- The coders of the plant – "internal" characteristics.

- Persons with control of workplaces – the manager who orders/creates a scope of robot use.

- Manufacturers, importers and suppliers of the plant/robot – the salesperson who helps you choose and pick the right robot.

- Persons who install, erect or make ANY changes to the plant – the delivery/coder who provides the initial start destination for your robot.

The challenges at the front end may be able to be somewhat simplified for delivery of new robots in your workplace. However, you should request this Safety in Design requirement in your order as, if they don't deliver to you, your company will still be required to share it with the lawmakers in your area.

When we look back at how changes in the workplace were responded to just a few years ago, for any crews let alone a unionised workforce, something as simple as a change of food supplier (e.g. shifting form Coca-Cola® products to Pepsi® products) could mean a strike.

Payrates not increasing by 4% each annum could mean action by a collective group of staff.

Therefore, we expect we will have some work to do to make sure we carefully and considerately plan and evolve our workforces into the new ways of work.

It is possible that, in the future, our Humanoid Robots will also be able to take action or strike. Their "electronic personhood" status means that we could be reviewing and advising on appropriate and inappropriate interactions of staff and robot conduct.

Given the liveliness of some of first, best-funded and most-advanced humanoids, we could be looking at sexual harassment between human and humanoids. Would it be okay for business leaders to only employ humanoids that look like Samantha designed by Sergi Santos of Synth Amatus.

The design / hire of new Humanoids will have to align with the same levels of ethics, dress code and presentation as with other staff.

A whole new world unravels and currently our law does not specifically prescribe details on how businesses should approach this.

Insurance Impacts for Fewer Humans More Humanoids

There will be insurance pool impacts to insurers as, with less insured Human Units, it is expected that premiums will rise to compensate.

After this position is established, businesses will find premiums very problematic for human employment and will either take one of two options: 1) employ fewer people, with more robotic replacement; or 2) push back against the insurance companies for a reduction in unsustainable market pricing.

It's is our belief that this pushback will lead to insurance companies pushing for global Humanoid Robotic insurable units.

The insurance may be based upon the cost of sustained company damage by employee Damage Costs, the same salary value as a replaced set of humans for the process it now undertakes or the price of replacement, like with car insurance.

The pool will need to refill as people will still be requiring benefits as employees or gig workers who would be deemed employees at the time of an incident.

Governments are already exploring taxation of Robots to help pay for the lost taxes from employees that would normally pay for collective services provided by the government.

In our view, insurers will not lose their pie; they will evolve to make new products for better coverage, starting with Robot Policies & Gig Worker Policies, which are already starting to emerge.

According to McKinsey & Company, globally it is expected that up to 375 million people will need to reskill. During this time, they will most likely be unemployed and not contributing to taxation or insurance pools.

Globally, up to 375 million workers may need to switch occupational categories.

Number of workers needing to move out of current occupational category to go find work, 2016-30 (trendline scenario)[1]

■ Midpoint automation   ■ Additional from rapid automation adoption (each block = 1 million workers)

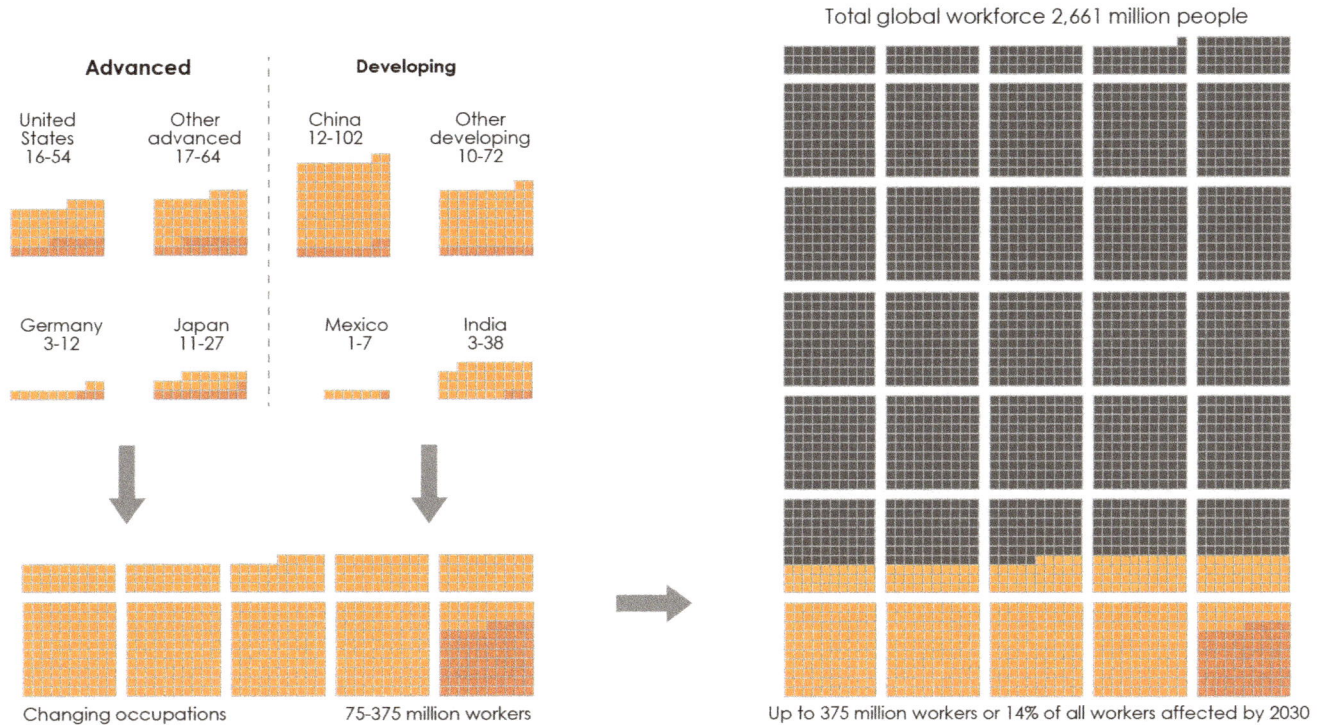

Advanced

United States
16-54

Other advanced
17-64

Germany
3-12

Japan
11-27

Developing

China
12-102

Other developing
10-72

Mexico
1-7

India
3-38

Changing occupations   75-375 million workers

Total global workforce 2,661 million people

Up to 375 million workers or 14% of all workers affected by 2030

1 some occupational data projected into 2016 baseline from latest available 2014 data

McKinsey&Company | Source: US Bureau of Labor Statistic; McKinsey Global Institute analysis

Unfortunately, we believe the response of the insurance companies could be delayed if there aren't global discussions soon. The reaction will be prolonged, as they won't be jumping to reduce premiums at any point.

Humanoid Rights in Workers Compensation and Legal Space

As the year moves forward after we have installed our Humanoid Robot, we now have some new risks and opportunities ahead.

As the business and people have more and more interactions, both people and Humanoids, we expect legal activity to commence, including legal cases where Humanoid Robots are parties.

When you appoint "Electronic Personhood" in practice, you are saying that this robot could be found to have breached a law or duty. That means any laws or duties that would be appointed to a person/human.

This will create a whole new view.

When Manage Damage surveyed more than 200 business leaders in Australia, they found that only 13.33% considered that Robots/AI would never be considered as a "Worker"/Employee/Person.

We found that more than 33% considered it likely or definite that that Robots/AI would be considered as a "Worker"/Employee/Person.

When asking our survey participants if a Robot could or would be deemed an "Officer"/Boss/Supervisor/Person, more than 20% considered it likely or definite that that Robots/AI would be considered as a "Officer"/Boss/ Supervisor/Person.

When exploring responsibility and accountability for legal actions, we asked participants about a hypothetical scenario in which a driver-less car has accidently struck a pedestrian in an attempt to save its user from a collision. Participants were then asked to provide their thoughts on who would hold legal liability in this situation.

The response was very akin to that of a "plant" view, with their expectation for responsibility tending towards the car manufacturer, owner and designer of the auto-piloted car.

When considering Humanoid Robots, it is a different level, as according to the design, a humanoid robot can think for itself and learn. If given "Electronic Personhood" status, why would they be allowed to continue to "live" without consequences for their actions?

Need for Assistance for Managing Artificial Intelligence Technologies in the Workplace

93% of businesses surveyed said that AI is not addressed properly in today's regulatory landscape.

Businesses want help to manage this new risk for business and people.

Business would like to see documents that can be used to aid employers in defining and managing the risk of AI and Robotics; in particular, when surveyed, they were very interested in:

- Practical documents for assessing and managing AI
- Guidelines and factsheets of legal requirements for AI duties and risks
- Assistance & advice from coding specialists

Currently, since our governments worldwide are struggling, we need to work from a simple approach: they are "plant" but the "plant" has a more complex design. We need to approach the uses, intentions and supply chain as a full view and inch-by-inch – byte-by-byte – your new robot can be safely installed into your business.

Conclusion:

The approach for safety and risk management in the future will be vastly different. Fresh and different thinking must be used to provide some revitalised models to help business approach and manage the new risks and opportunities.

Smart effective AI advantages will change the way we live, think and work. Safety and risk managers need to understand these new ways and work with our new "plant" to make sure we still provide for the health and safety of the people and the humanoid robots who we will call our friends.

APPENDIX
INTERVIEW

Interview with Jillian L Hamilton on Robotics & AI

LIAM KELLY

Jillian Hamilton Interview Transcript

LK: Today I'm going to look for some of your opinions regarding emerging Artificial Intelligence Technologies, such as where we can expect them to be in the next 5-10 years in a number of different areas, such as in the insurance industry, but also the greater legal repercussions. To start off, how do you define Artificial Intelligence?

JH: So to clarify something for you, I see the issue of insurance / legal as both being encompassed by risk. For me the key element and driver for us doing the AI piece at Manage Damage is that it is becoming part of the way we work, so ignoring robotics and Artificial Intelligence in the industry as it enters our businesses is like putting your head in the sand and saying "I don't want to deal with a very large risk to our business". So I have decided that we would explore that from the legal aspects, where robots may become officers and are being deemed as persons – as is beginning to be spoken about in the EU – as well as the insurable view of robots and intelligence, because it has a financial outcome, and also how we can provide solutions to employers/businesses.

For me, Artificial Intelligence is decisions being made and processes being done without humans interacting or physically doing. Excluding humans for some of the highest risk tasks is normally where AI and robotics have commenced in our business workplace. In the past it was just plant – it was just a machine – but our machines have gotten so clever now, so instead of just having machines doing heavy lifting, they can now do more things in the workplace. So Artificial Intelligence has many definitions; people forget that our mobile phones are Artificial Intelligence: we don't have to spell anymore, suggestions are made when we search for things. So AI is using computers, electronics and technology to do tasks that usually the brain would Figure out, or a human would complete. So that's how I define AI.

LK: Do you feel like businesses today are adequately prepared for the risks associated with emerging AI technologies?

JH: At the moment it's my fear that businesses are ignoring the AI technology from one or two fronts. Smart businesses are exploring the opportunities of AI for cost reductions, risk reductions, and as robots get smarter they are being trusted more to do work in the workplace. In Australia we are behind, we have always explored new technologies slower than other nations and unfortunately if you look at the innovation scales from worldwide surveys, Australia is behind New Zealand. So we have a lot of work to do and that's why our government is spending millions of dollars trying to encourage people to do research on new innovations for businesses for Australia to be smarter and more productive. So in summary, I don't believe businesses or the government are ready. I think that some businesses are ignorant to the speed that robots will be replacing a lot of their employees work, so I think that some businesses are exploring options to save money, but other businesses are either being naïve or deliberately not being consulted. Studies are showing that up to 40% of employees could be replaced by robots in the future, so this has a lot of impact on our economy. I think that businesses are frightened to explore it properly, and quite rightly, because whenever there is a replacement of a human with a robot it has a lot of costs and also a lot of ethical challenges.

LK: Following up from that, you seem to be under the impression that robots will take over to some predominant degree in the workforce. What do you think will be the state of AI and robotics technology in the next ten years?

JH: I think there's going to be a couple of waves. Like off-shoring, some people had really good wins and some had gigantic failures, and I think this will happen with AI and robotics as well, because people will make good and bad decisions on installation and use of robotics and AI. I think that people could potentially use bad change management, and just start using AI without proper consultation of the workforce, production teams, or senior management. I think that will also have a gigantic impact on how people view businesses, and from a corporate/social responsibility, there are going to be a lot of businesses with protest signs about. People are going to be quite disappointed.

LK: So the biggest risk for businesses is that they will roll out technologies that they may not fully understand?

JH: Yeah, the first thing is complete lack of understanding, not only of robotics and Artificial Intelligence, which is a special area of computing and programming. There is a worldwide shortage of computer operators and programmers at this stage. I believe that we currently do not have enough people skilled or being reskilled in AI and robotics including specifically repairers and programmers who have skills, capacity and foresight to build robots. There is a known lack of supply of programmers worldwide and building a computer program is very different to building a walking talking acting, thinking doing robot. If that is the case and 40% of all working roles is going to be replaced by AI, my concern is we're not going to have enough programmers, we're not going to have enough people understanding what programmers do, and we're going to have a lot of people with a heap of junk AI products with very little service; I think we could be buying robots who then need servicing and attention and then we will have to wait a long time to get service to repair, adjust, build or recode the robots. This could be critical to high production businesses who would be relying on robots to produce product. that will have trouble meeting the OHS legal requirements for new plant or robotics. I think our regulators are unprepared for what robotics means for the legal system. I know currently there's only theoretical discussions about whether a robot makes decisions or not and what is the implications of this to the legal outcomes and I know that people are uninsured for this. So my fear is a complete lack of preparation, which is why we undertake these particular research projects on AI and robotics because we want people to be able to have the tools to be able to safely enter a robot into the workplace, but also safely manage the inclusion of AI to the workplace, and also the exclusion of staff.

How long do you think it will take for Artificial Intelligence to become the predominant form of worker as opposed to humans?

JH: I think our technology has moved at a pace of knots. It was only a few years ago that phones were the size of a brick, now they are small, can fit in your pockets and can do a full suite of work, so the speed of technology change and design is very fast, and robotics have improved at the same rate. Whether it will continue to improve at this rate depends on how much use, so whether businesses take on and properly installs these robotic plans into their workplace. It's my fear that unless we are properly prepared that it won't be done well and will ultimately have a massive negative impact for businesses and society. I think that change management is critical at this stage as you need to consider what shall we do with the people who are not longer required for employment; but we need help from our Governments globally to help reskill people. As a result there may even be a complete revert away from AI. Also, from an ethics point of view there's a lot of businesses who don't want to replace all their employees with robots, and that ethical position and stance is going to be very challenging, particularly for family businesses. In summary, in ten years' time I think we would have been a long way into robotics, but I think it might go out again and revert to "old fashioned, hand crafted, one of a kind sales of items as a niche product to buy, make yourself feel good buy a product made by a person rather than a robot, it might be how charities make money in the future? It's also my fear that Robotic installation could go so well, that unless you're in the top 10 or 20% of learning and development, you're going to be on the UBI (Universal Basic Income), which effectively means up to 40% of our population is on social benefits – our governments can not afford this today and most certainly would not be able to afford it in the future when they are collecting less taxes. It has the potential to create a rift in society, a rift between those working and not working, not rich and poor; employed and unemployed, consider all the tasks identified as replacement now not working – these are our "Workers" what will they do; this kind could cruicially divide people and will create much civil unrest.

LK: So would you say that overall your optimistic that AI and robotic technology will be advantageous overall or do you think it could create such an upset that people will turn away from the technology altogether?

I think it's going to create a huge economic hole, and that's my greatest fear. We need to Figure out what to do with all the humans. We have a problem where instead of having 10% on the dole, we'll have 30 or 40% of people on the dole. They could become a part of society that can't afford to pay their house loans, and that could become an economic disaster. So I'm worried that we may face an economic downturn that will only improve things for the 10 or 20 percenters. So it's going to make a very poor society, and I think that is 5 – 10 years from now, and is super dangerous for our life, our living, our security, our society and our macro-economies, these people can easily be our friends, sisters, brothers, husbands or wives.

LK: So what do you think about the idea of heavy taxation for businesses who are monopolising on AI technologies?

JH: There needs to be a tax on the human replacement by the robots, because if they're not taxed and insured, how are we to gather the funds to run our governments and society, and pay for all the people on the social security benefits? So if there's 40% fewer earners, there's 40% more people wanting the dole, and that is a large amount of money that we need to find in an economy that's already at a deficit. If you take out a human and you put in a robot, then potentially we should be taxing the individual robots because we need to make money to pay for the humans that are left without jobs. I think it's unfair that the 10 or 20 percenters could be facing 70% tax – I think that's unfair, but I can't see a new line of jobs being created. I can't see what you would do with an additional 40% of workers who are not employed.

LK: How do you think legislation will have to change to keep pace with AI?

JH: We've got to improve the knowledge of the people that make decisions around risk. So when people are writing legislation, they need to be using IT consultants and AI specialists to be able to write their legislation with robotics in mind. So when they write legislations, standards and processes they need to keep that in mind. When I look at Safe Work Australia, and all of the regulators in all of the states, all of the regulations are currently written with only humans in mind. One of the processes that we have undertaken is to do a review of the legislation so that if you were to replace the word "person" with "robot" and to determine how that would impact the legislation. There's a code of practice due for AI, robotics and how that can be managed in the workplace and that's something we're looking forward to designing, scoping and creating.

LK: How do you think AI will impact the insurance industry specifically?

JH: I think that AI will cause an absolute disaster in the insurance zone. There's a few things: one, it's going to be very hard for insurance companies to make the profits they currently are without significantly increasing the costs to current employers, which pushes them further into preferring robotic technologies. It would also change how insurance would be quoted, managed, and marked. You would insure a set of robots so that if it breaks down it can have maintenance and repair, but I think people will try to get out of it if they are individually taxing or insuring robots. I think there are going to be a lot of broke insurance companies, and that we might see more boutique, and different kinds of insurers arrive. The insurance area needs to move to low-base, value-base models, and their model is the complete opposite right now, so I predict many going bankrupt, because there's so many pay-outs at the moment, and there'll be huge pay-outs going through as AI technology increases, because the staff will make claims and the costs will increase significantly, which will make businesses go bust and they won't have the money to go to the insurance industry.

Do you have any fear of AI gaining sentience or developing goals that are misaligned with humanity?

I don't think it's the robots that would harm anyone; I think it's the hackers. I think our greatest global risk is having our robot workforces and automated processes being hacked, and I think that will be a reality. If you want to create a really large amount of chaos, you go and irreplaceably damage "the cloud" , the place where people think their data and security is being kept, while in reality it's not in a "cloud" it's in someones' gigantic storage place somewhere probably in a paddock in a remote location in the desert somewhere, that is where true unrest and havoc would be created.

.

APPENDIX
LEGISLATIVE REVIEW

Shortfalls of Legislation Regarding Artificial Intelligence & Humanoid Robotics

L KELLY & J L HAMILTON

The table below explains the major Artificial Intelligence Categories, their uses, their risks, controls and the protections available. Manage Damage Team Member Liam Kelly produced this.

ARTIFICIAL INTELLIGENCE RISK IDENTIFICATION AND POSSIBLE CONTROLS & PROTECTIONS

AI Technology	Description / Possible uses	Risks of use	Potential Controls	Protections available
1. Mobile Phones / Smart Devices	Storage of personal information and contacts, as well as internet search history and social media activity	Hackers could obtain personal information or tap into device systems such as cameras or microphones	Review any security permissions granted to third party apps prior to installation	Keep devices updated for security purposes Use password protection for accessing device
2. Social Media	Social media services use AI to selectively filter news and advertisements to the user	Overexposure to information that has been specifically selected to tailor to individual biases	Consider alternate sources for information rather than just a social media news feed	Review security settings to avoid potential privacy concerns
		Privacy concerns regarding notificatio pop-up	Use different passwords for social media services. Never share account information	Seek out social media alternatives that place greater emphasis on privacy and personal security
3. GPS	GPS systems utilise AI that factor in traffic data to determine ideal routes	GPS history can be reviewed to determine previous destinations	Review GPS history and delete entries	Use trusted GPS applica-tions on secure device
		Certain systems may be susceptible to hacking		
4. Spam filtering	Google's spam filtering employs AI to review content of emails so they can be categorised	Privacy concerns regarding Google analysing and storing the content of every email received	If concerned, consider alternate email services that place greater emphasis on privacy	Google will permanently delete stored emails after deletion of the account

5. Search engines	Search engines use AI to filter and select most relevant results	Priority of results can be manipulated through search engine optimisation Certain search engines may censor or hide relevant links Search engine history can easily be reviewed by anyone using the same device	Review search engine history and delete entries	Consider alternate sources of information or alternate search engines if you suspect manipulation of results
6. Driver-less cars	Driver-less cars use AI and sensory technologies to drive without a user	Collision due to systems error or mismatched priorities (i.e., car may veer off-road to avoid a collision but inadvertently cause more damage)	Passively observe driver-less cars activities and intervene if it is about to perform an unsafe action	Do not use current driverless technologies until they have been determined to be reliable. Emergency stop systems
7. Automated machines	Automated machines use AI and sensory technologies to perform work without the need for a user	Damage or injury due to malfunction or corrupted priorities	Perform risk assessment on automated technology to determine potential risks to worker safety	Only utilise automated machinery that has been certified for safe use
8. Robots	Robots are a form of mobile automated machine that uses AI and sensory technology	Damage or injury due to malfunction or corrupted priorities	Perform risk assessment on robots to determine risks to safety Perform continuous assessments over course of lifetime	Emergency stop systems Use robots certified for safe use Discuss safety concerns with designer/manufacturer

LEGISLATION REVIEW: WORK HEALTH AND SAFETY ACT 2011 (QLD)

Liam Kelly of Manage Damage created the following table, which highlights the current shortfalls of today's legislation structures. To acknowledge Artificial Intelligence and Humanoid Robotics in the workplace, the Queensland Work Health and Safety Act has been developed by the Model Act for Occupational Health and Safety for Australia, and thus has a number of similarities to other Australian State legislation.

SECTION	DESCRIPTION	SHORTFALL FOR AI	ISSUES	RECOMMENDATIONS AND SOLUTIONS
S7 - Meaning of worker	Outlines the current definition of workers	No mention of AI or electronic workers	Electronic personhood will likely need to be considered for certain work tasks	Addition of: (a) the type of worker (human or electronic)
S8 - Meaning of workplace	Outlines the current definition of workplace	Does not mention workplace AI	Large AI systems could be considered workplaces. (e.g., vehicles can be considered workplaces; do driverless vehicle workplaces then count as an AI workplace?)	Additional requirements regarding the operation and management within AI workplaces
S10 - Act binds all persons	Specifies that the Act applies to all persons (inc. businesses, State, & the Common-wealth)	Need to apply Act to AI / robotic systems to enable workplace use	If AI is not bound by the Act then there are difficulties in determining liability	Specify that the Act binds all persons including AI / robotic systems
S17 - Manage-ment of risks	Outlines the requirements for the manage-ment of workplace risks	Does not consider AI technologies to aid in manage-ment of risk	AIs will likely be able to identify risks that are undetectable to normal persons	Addition of a requirement to use risk-identifying AIs in high-risk workplace environments Addition of requirements to address identified risks from specialised AIs

Section	Current Outline	Gap	Impact	Recommendation
S19 - Primary Duty of Care	Outlines the PCBUs duties to ensure that risk to workers is minimised	No mention of duties of AI / robotics if they are in a supervisory role (officer)	Officer AIs would be required to uphold the duties outlined in this section	Specify that the Primary Duty of Care applies to AI / Robots. Expand section relating to the safe use, handling, and storage of plant to include AI / robots.
S20 - Duty of persons conducting businesses or undertakings involving management or control of workplaces	Outlines the duties of the person with management control of a workplace	No mention of duties of AI / robotics if they are in a supervisory role (officer)	Officer AIs would be required to uphold the duties outlined in this section	Specify that the duties outlined in this section apply to officer AI / Robots.
S21 - Duty of persons conducting businesses or undertakings involving management or control of fixtures, fittings or plant at workplaces	Outlines the duties regarding management of control of fixtures, fittings or plant	Does not include workplace management of AI or robots. No mention of duties of officer AI / Robots	AI / Robotics will have unique management requirements from plant and will need to be addressed separately	Additional specifications regarding the management of AI systems and robots
S22 - Duties of persons conducting businesses or undertakings that design plant, substances or structures	Outlines the duties regarding the design of plant, substances or structures	Does not include the duties regarding the design of AI or robots	AI / Robotics will have unique design requirements compared to plant	Additional specifications regarding the design of AI systems and robots
S23 - Duties of persons conducting businesses or undertakings that manufacture plant, substances or structures	Outlines the duties regarding manufacture of control of fixtures, fittings or plant	Does not include the duties regarding the manufacture of AI or robots	AI / Robotics will have unique manufacturing requirements compared to plant	Additional specifications regarding the manufacture of AI systems and robots
S24 - Duties of persons conducting businesses or undertakings that import plant, substances or structure	Outlines the duties regarding the importing of control of fixtures, fittings or plant	Does not include the duties regarding the importing of AI or robots	AI / Robotics will have unique importing requirements compared to plant	Additional specifications regarding the importing of AI systems and robots

Section				
S25 - Duties of persons conducting businesses or undertakings that supply plant, substances or structures	Outlines the duties regarding the supply of fixtures, fittings or plant	Does not include the duties regarding supply of AI or robots	AI / Robotics will have unique supply requirements compared to plant	Additional specifications regarding the supply of AI systems and robots
S26 - Duty of persons conducting businesses or undertakings that install, construct or commission plant or structures	Outlines the duties regarding the installation of control of fixtures, fittings or plant	Does not include duties regarding installation of AI or robots	AI / Robotics will have unique installation requirements compared to plant	Additional specifications regarding the installation of AI systems and robots
S27 - Duties of officers	Specifies the duties of officers and requirement to exercise due diligence in carrying out duties	Does not include duties for electronic officers	AI / Robotic can exercise due diligence in carrying out duties listed in this section	Include "electronic officers" to have the same duties as listed in this section
S28 - Duties of workers	Specifies the duties of workers to take reasonable care for their own safety and others	No mention of duties of AI/robotics as workers	These duties will apply if AIs are considered electronic persons	Wording in this section does not need to be changed so long as workers include electronic persons
Division 5 - Offences and Penalties (incl. S30-34)	Expands on the penalties applied upon failure to uphold duties	Does not consider penalties for non-human persons	There is a need to consider penalties for damages caused by AI / Robots as well as circumstances of dual liability between duty holders	Introduction of a new class of penalties that considers input from the designer, manufacturer, importer, or supplier (or other persons) to determine liability

S42 - Requirements for authorisation of plant or substance	Outlines the requirements regarding permitted use of plant	No mention regarding the use of unauthorised / regulated AI or robot systems	There will likely be certain classes of AI / Robotic systems that are regulated or require authorisation for use	An additional section or addendum to the current requirement to specify the requirements for authorisation of AI / Robots New guides will have to be written that cover the ethics and safety in design for robots and AI systems
S46 - Duty to consult with other duty holders	Outlines the requirement for consultation, coordination and cooperation between persons with the same duties	Does not specify requirements for duty holders to consult with regards to AI / Robotics	The requirements for manufacturers, designers, importers, and suppliers will extend to AI / Robotics	Wording in this section may not need to be altered, but the specific duties of described parties will need to be well-understood by those who wish to use AI / Robotics Consider duty to consult to workers on the installation of robotics
S50 - Request for election of health and safety representative	Specifies that workers may elect one or more health and safety representatives	Does not consider health and safety representative as electronic persons	AI / Robotics could fulfil the role of health & safety representative in workplace. Workers may request advice or assistance from AI representatives	Specify that AIs / Robotics can fulfil the requirements of Health & Safety Representatives and may be required to fulfil this role in high-risk workplaces.
S51 - Determination of work groups	Outlines the requirement for PCBUs to establish work groups upon request	No consideration regarding the creation of AI work groups	AI / Robotics work groups may be established within the workplace (and may be required for sufficiently hazardous activites)	Addition of a specification that AI / Robots can be ordered into work groups

Division 4 Health and Safety committees (inc. S60-67)	Outlines the requirement for the PCBU tion to establish a health and safety committee	No considera- tion regarding role of AI in health and safety commit- tees	High-risk industries may require AI / Robotic workers to provide input in Health and Safety committees	Inclusion of a potential require- ment for a special- ized AI / Robot to be included in Health and Safety Committees	Otherwise language can stay the same but consideration must be made for increased role of AI in Health & Safety representation
Division 5 Issue Resolution (inc. S80-82)	Outlines the requirements with regards to issue resolution (i.e., resolving and disputes relating to workplace health & safety)	No considera- tion for role of AI workers and potential disputes between electronic and human personnel	Considerations will have to be made regarding how AI / Robotics will factor into issue resolution	Disputes will likely need to be mediated by a human representa- tive on behalf of the AI / Robotic system	Legal precedence may need to be set before it is clear how these issues will normally be resolved
Division 6 Right to cease or direct cessation of unsafe work (inc. S83-89)	Outlines the situations in which workers can refuse to perform work that may pose a risk to their health & safety	Does not consider the role of AI risk identifiers and what work being carried out is unsafe	As stated, AI / Robotics may be better equipped to determine whether work being carried out is unsafe	An additional specification that specialised AI / Robots may be able to direct cessation of unsafe work if it is determined	

LEGISLATION REVIEW: WORK HEALTH AND SAFETY REGULATION 2011 (QLD)

Liam Kelly of Manage Damage created the following table, which highlights the current shortfalls of today's legislation structures. To acknowledge Artificial Intelligence and Humanoid Robotics in the Workplace, the Queensland Work Health and Safety Regulation has been developed by the Model Regulation for Occupational Health and Safety for Australia, and thus has a number of similarities to other Australian State legislation.

SECTION	DESCRIPTION	SHORTFALL FOR AI	ISSUES	RECOMMENDATIONS AND SOLUTIONS
S8 - Meaning of Supply	Defines supply as not including persons who do not control the supply or have authority over the supply	There are duties for supply of plant that would be expected to extend to supply of AI	Must consider specific duties that apply to the suppliers of AI / Robots	Potential specifications of unique requirements regarding supply of AI / Robots. Otherwise language in this section can remain the same
S17 - Matters to be taken into account in negotiations [with regards to work groups]	Outlines the requirements involved in specifying and determining work groups	No mention of AI / Robotic work groups	AI / Robotic work groups will likely be required for high-risk workplaces	It is expected that determination of work groups would require specifying whether the worker is electronic, ie: • (a)the type of worker (human or lectronic)
S23 - Default Procedure [with regards to Issue Resolution]	Outlines the procedures required in issue resolution	No mention of role of AI / Robots in issue resolution	Unique procedures for disputes between electronic and human workers will need to be determined	Additional specifications regarding procedures to be carried out between human and electronic workers. AIs will likely need to be represented by a human for these matters
S35 - Management of risk	Outlines the requirements for PCBUs to manage risk as far as is reasonably practicable	No mention of the role of AI / Robots in risk identification	Specialised AI / Robotic systems may be able to identify and manage risk that are undetectable by regular human workers	The language in this section can remain the same, but consideration should be made regarding risks identified by AI / robot workers and the requirements for PCBUs to adhere to their recommendations

S36 - Hierarchy of Control Measures	Provides an overview of the accepted hierarchy of control measures for managing risk (Elimination, substitution, isolation, engineering controls, administrative controls, PPE)	No mention of AI / Robot systems as a potential engineering control	Specialised AI / Robotic systems may be able to make determinations regarding the best application of the hierarchy of control measures	Use of AI in risk management may be considered an engineering control, but also may fall under its own category as it may become indispensable in certain high-risk industries
S37 - Maintenance of control measures	Outlines the requirements for the maintenance of control measures used to minimise risk	No mention of requirement to maintain AI control if it is used as a control measure to minimise risk	AIs / Robots being used as an engineering control will likely require maintenance to ensure they are operational	Additional specification to ensure that AI controls are being maintained so as to ensure their correct operation
S38 - Review of control measures	States the requirements for a PCBU to review and update control measures if required	Does not consider the role of AI in review of control measures	Specialised AI / Robots will likely review control measures more efficiently than human workers	Additional specification for PCBUs to employ AIs in review of control measures for high-risk workplaces
S39 - Information, training and instruction	Outlines requirements to ensure that workers receive adequate training regarding the nature of their work	Does not specify training requirements for electronic persons	AI / Robotic workers will likely need to be trained in specific tasks, but the method of teaching them may differ	Potential introduction of "training data" that can be uploaded into AI systems to qualify them for an area of work. Additional specifications regarding unique requirements for electronic workers may need to be outlined under this section
S42 - Duty to provide first aid	Outlines the requirements for PCBUs to ensure that workers can receive first aid in the event of an incident	Does not consider the role of AI in applying or receiving first aid	Specialised AI/Robots may be able to perform first aid procedures on site.	Electronic workers who have been damaged may have their own "first aid" requirements, though this may just be considered maintenance/repairs

Section		Limitation	Opportunity / Damage	Recommendation
S43 – Duty to prepare, maintain and implement emergency plan	States the requirements for a PCBU to implement an emergency plan for the workplace	Does not consider the role of AI /robotic systems in the development of emergency plans; Does not consider the role of AI / Robotic systems in carrying out emergency plans	Damage AI/Robots may have unique requirements for "first aid" or repair; AI / Robotic systems may be able to analyse and determine best course of action with regards to development of emergency plans; Certain classes of AI / Robot may be able to mount rescues in the event of an emergency	For high-risk industries, it may be necessary to include a requirement for first aid robots to be available in the event of an incident; An additional stated requirement for emergency AI / Robotic systems for high-risk workplaces
S44 – Provision to workers and use of personal protective equipment	States the requirements of the PCBU to ensure that PPE is provided to workers	Does not consider PPE requirements for robotic systems.	Certain robotics / AI systems may be exempt from PPE requirements, or they may have their own unique PPE requirements (e.g., water protection)	Expansion of this section to include consideration for AI / Robotic personnel and their PPE requirements or lack thereof
S48 – Remote or isolated work	Outlines requirements for remote or isolated work (inc. specification to be able to communicate with worker in isolation)	Does not consider role of AI / Robotics in remote or isolated work	Robots / AI will likely have different requirements with regards to isolated work. Psychosocial stressors are not expected to apply to AI / Robots	A potential requirement for work that requires extreme isolation to be carried out by an electronic worker rather than a human.
S49 - Ensuring Exposure standards for substances etc. not exceeded	Outlines the requirements to ensure exposure standards to a hazardous substance is not exceeded	Does not consider role of AI / Robotics in workplace monitoring and	Robots / AI can use sensors that will allow them to continuously monitor the workplace	A potential requirement for workplaces that utilise hazardous materials to employ AI / Robots who are able to perform workplace monitoring and direct

Section	Description	Consideration	AI / Robotics implications	Notes / recommendations
S50 - Monitoring airborne contaminant levels	determining exposure levels		Robots / AI may be exempt from work if conditions become unsafe if they are unharmed by airborne contaminants	direct cessation of work if conditions become unsafe; A specification for electronic workers to be exempt from safety requirements if it is determined they would not be harmed by airborne contaminants
S51 - Managing risks to health and safety [with regards to hazardous atmospheres]	Outlines the requirements to determine if an atmosphere is hazardous and determining safe atmospheric levels	Does not consider role of AI / Robotics in determining safe atmospheric levels	Robots / AIs can use sensors that can determine oxygen levels as well as concentration of potential poisons / contaminants in the atmosphere	A potential requirement to use specialised monitoring AIs in workplaces where the atmosphere may become hazardous; An exemption for electronic workers who would not be harmed by hazardous atmospheres
S54 - Management of requirements of PCBUs to manage the risk of falling objects in the workplace	Outlines the requirements of PCBUs to manage the risk of falling objects risks	Does not consider role of AI / Robotics in identifying risks; Does not consider role of AI / Robots in posing a risk as a falling object	Robotic systems could pose a risk to workers if they topple and injure human personnel; Robotic systems could also identify and manage potential falling hazards	Language in this section can likely remain the same; however PCBUs must consider the risk of AI / Robotic workers based on their size and the jobs they are performing (e.g., whether they are working at height)
S57 - Managing risk of hearing loss from noise	Outlines the requirements for PCBUs to manage the risk of hearing loss of hearing loss to workers	Does not consider role of AI in monitoring sound level	AIs with sensors can determine overall sound exposure.; AIs / Robotics will likely have different requirements with regards to acceptable levels of sound exposure	Consider a requirement for noise-sensing AIs to monitor workplace noise and direct cessation of work if unsafe; This section may also need to specify an exemption from the requirement to manage noise exposure to AIs if it is

				deemed they will be unharmed from the exposure
S60 - Managing risks to health and safety [from hazardous manual tasks]	Outlines the requirements for PCBUs to manage risk of musculoskeletal disorders emerging from hazardous manual tasks	Does not consider the unique role of AI / Robots in performing hazardous manual tasks	Certain AI/Robots will be able to perform hazardous manual tasks with significantly reduced risk of damage compared to humans	Consider a requirement for robots to perform hazardous manual tasks that have been associated with the development of a musculoskeletal disorder.
S61 - Duties of designers, manufacturers, importers and suppliers of plant or structures	Outlines the duties that apply to designers, manufacturers, importers and suppliers of plant	Does not mention duties relating to AI / Robotics	The requirements of the listed duty holders can be expected to extend to AI systems	Additional specifications are required in this section that specify the duties of designers, manufacturers, importers, and suppliers of AI / robotic systems
Part 4.3 - Confined Space	This part defines "confined space" and outlines the various responsibilities PCBUs have to ensure worker safety in these conditions	Does not consider role of AI / Robotics in confined spaces. No mention of electronic persons	AI / Robotics can be expected to perform work in confined space without serious risk to themselves	Work in confined spaces may need to be restricted to AI / Robotic systems in sufficiently hazardous situations.
Part 4.5 - High risk work	This part defines "high risk work" and outlines the various responsibilities PCBUs have to ensure worker safety in these conditions	Does not consider role of AI / Robotics in performing high risk work. No mention of electronic persons	AI / Robotic work groups may be required to undertake high-risk work instead of human personnel due to their ability to withstand certain conditions	It may be necessary to specify that only electronic personnel can perform high-risk work in situations where it has been determined that they are not at significant risk of being damaged
S167 - Diving Work	Outlines the requirements for persons performing diving work	Does not consider role of electronic workers who can withstand diving conditions	Specialised diving robots may be employed to perform high-risk work due to their unique requirements	An exemption for the requirements for AI / Robotics under this section and an outline of new requirements (i.e., the robot must be designed specifically for designing and must be able to be trained)

S168 - Person conducting business or undertaking business or performing diving work must ensure fitness of workers [with regards to diving]	Outlines specific fitness requirements for persons who can perform diving work	Does not consider role of electronic workers who can withstand diving conditions	Specialised robots will not need to demonstrate human fitness to perform diving work	An exemption for the requirements for AI / Robotics under this section and an outline of new requirements (i.e., the robot must be designed specifically for designing and must be able to be trained)
Part 5.1 - General duties for plant and structures	This part outlines the general requirements with regards to plant and structures	No mention of AI / Robots	The duties of plant under this section should also apply to AI / Robotics	Introduction of a new part of an addendum to this section that covers the General duties for AI and Robots
S187 - Provision of information to manufacturer	Specifies the requirements of the plant designer to consult with the plant manufacturer regarding associated risks	No mention of AI / Robots	The duties of plant under this should also apply to AI / Robotics	Requirements for the provision of information between designer and manufacturer will need to be established for AI / Robots (Likely based on an extension of the plant requirements listed in this section)
S188 - Hazard identified in design during manufacture	Specifies the requirements for manufacturers to communicate with designers in the event of identified hazards during manufacture	No mention of AI / Robots	The duties of plant under this should also apply to AI / Robotics	Requirements for the provision of information between designer and manufacturer will need to be established for AI / Robots
S193 - Control of risks [regarding undertakings that manufacture plant]	Specifies the duties to control of risk that apply to manufacturers of plant	No mention of AI / Robots	The duties of plant under this should also apply to AI / Robotics	Requirements under this section are expected to extend to AI / Robotics and should have their own sections or addendums to address this

Section	Description			
S196 – Information to be obtained and provided by importer	Specifies the information that importers must take reasonable steps to obtain	No mention of AI / Robots	The duties of plant under this should also apply to AI / Robotics	Requirements under this section are expected to extend to AI / Robotics and should be addressed in their own section
S197 – Control of risk [regarding importing of plant]	Specifies the duties to control risk that apply to importers of plant	No mention of AI / Robots	The duties of plant under this should also apply to AI / Robotics	Requirements under this section are expected to extend to AI / Robotics and should be addressed in their own section
S198 – Information to be obtained and provided by supplier	Specifies the information that suppliers must take reasonable steps to obtain	No mention of AI / Robots	The duties of plant under this should also apply to AI / Robotics	Requirements under this section are expected to extend to AI / Robotics and should be addressed in their own section
S199 – Supply of second-hand plant - duties of supplier	Outlines the requirements for suppliers of second-hand plant to take reasonable steps to identify faults and provide written notice of the condition of the plant	No mention of AI / Robots	The duties of plant under this should also apply to AI / Robotics	Requirements under this section are expected to extend to AI / Robotics and should be addressed in their own section
S200 – Second-hand plant to be used for scrap or spare parts	Outlines the requirements to specify that second-hand plant must be used for scrap before supply	No mention of AI / Robots	The duties of plant under this should also apply to AI / Robotics. Potential ethical considerations may eventually be necessary when considering disposal of AI / robots	Requirements under this section are expected to extend to AI / Robotics and should be addressed in their own section. Sufficiently intelligent robots / AIs may have their unique requirements regarding decommission / dismantling due to ethical concerns

S201 - Duties of persons conducting businesses or undertakings that install, construct or commission plant	Outlines the requirements for installation of plant to be in accordance with information provided by the manufacturer, supplier, designer, or importer of the plant	No mention of AI / Robots	The duties of plant under this section are expected to extend to AI / Robotics and should be addressed in their own section	Requirements under this section are expected to extend to AI / Robotics and should be addressed in their own section
S204 – Control of risks arising from installation or commissioning of plant	Specifies the duties to control risk that apply to installers or commissioners of plant	No mention of AI / Robots	The duties of plant under this should also apply to AI / Robotics	Requirements under this section are expected to extend to AI / Robotics and should be addressed in their own section
S205 - Preventing unauthor-ised management or control of plant at a workplace to prevent unauthorized alterations to plant	Outlines the requirement for the person with unauthor-ised management or control of plant at a workplace to prevent unauthorized alterations to plant	No mention of AI / Robots	The duties of plant under this section should also apply to AI / Robotics, though it may be difficult to determine what counts as plant alteration with machine -learning AIs, who are consistently learning from the environment to inform their behaviour	Consideration should be made for what exactly constitutes an unauthorized alteration to an AI or robotic system.
S206 - Proper use of plant and controls	Outlines the requirement for the person with management or control of plant to ensure that plant is being used correctly by persons	No mention of AI / Robots	AI / Robotics may not be "used" by workers as plant is. In this case the requirements listed in this section could apply to AI / Robots that appear to be acting beyond their usual parameters	A requirement to ensure that AI / Robotic systems are working according to specifications and are demonstrating no unusual outward behaviour

S211 - Emergency stops	Outlines the requirements for the person with management or control of plant to ensure the correct form of emergency stop are installed if necessary	No mention of AI / Robots	AI / Robotics will likely need an emergency stop function (potentially remote activated) if its actions are posing a risk to human workers, or if it is malfunctioning in any way that could cause harm	Requirement for the implementation of emergency stop systems for AI / Robots that could potentially cause harm to human workers
S212 - Warning devices	Outlines the requirements for the positioning of warning devices in a workplace if they are being used	No mention of AI / Robots	AI / Robots may be fitted with warning devices if it detects dangerous activities or is malfunctioning	Requirement for certain AI / Robotic systems to have in-built warning devices to alert workers
S213 - Maintenance and inspection of plant	Outlines the requirements for the person with management or control of plant to ensure that required maintenance and inspection is performed	No mention of AI / Robots	The duties of plant should also apply to AI / Robotics, though they will likely have unique requirements that distinguishes them from plant	Requirements under this section are expected to extend to AI / Robotics and should be addressed in their own section with additional considerations made regarding the persons required to perform maintenance and inspections
S214 - Powered mobile plant - general control of risk	Outlines the responsibility to determine that plant will not overturn, collide, or experience mechanical failure, as well as responsibility to determine that operators of plant are not at risk	No mention of AI / Robots	The duties of plant under this section should also apply to AI / Robotics, though it is unlikely that AI systems will often require human operators	Requirements under this section are expected to extend to AI / Robotics and should be addressed in their own section with potential alterations made regarding the control of risk for operators

S215 - Powered mobile plant - specific control measures	Outlines the specific actions to take to avoid potential risks outlined above	No mention of AI / Robots	The duties of plant under this section should also apply to AI / Robotics, though it is unlikely that AI systems will often require human operators	Requirements under this section are expected to extend to AI / Robotics and should be addressed in their own section with potential alterations made regarding the control of risk for operators
S219 - Plant that lifts or suspends loads	Outlines the requirements for the person with management or control of plant to manage risks associated with plant that lifts or suspends loads	No mention of AI / Robots	The duties of plant under this section also apply to to AI / Robotics (i.e., the robot must be designed to be able to lift or suspend loads)	Requirements under this section are expected to extend to AI / Robotics and should be addressed in their own section
S220 - Exception - Plant not specifically designed to lift or suspend a person	Outlines the requirements for lifting Plant or control of plant was not originally designed for that purpose	No mention of AI / Robots	Large AI systems will likely follow the same requirements for plant under this section	
S222 - Industrial Robots	Outlines the requirements for management of an industrial robot	No mention of AI / Robots	The role of robots in industry is expected to greatly expand and include additional risks to plant	Additional risks to consider include privacy concerns from AI monitoring, lack of maintenance resulting in malfunctions, environmental factors
S226 Plant with presence-sensing safeguarding system-records	Outlines the requirements for presence-sensing safeguards to be recorded, monitored, and maintained	No mention of AI / Robots	Robotic systems that contain moving parts that could be damaging to humans will likely utilise presence-sensing systems	The specifications outlined in this section of the regulations would also apply to Robotic presence-sensing systems

Section	Description			Additional specification
Part 5.2 – Additional duties relating to registered plant and plant designs	This part outlines the requirements for certain plant to be registered	No mention of AI / Robots	Certain AI / Robotic systems will likely require registration	Additional specification under this part concerning registration of AI / Robots
S228 – Records and information [with regards to Duty of person conducting a business or undertaking who designs plant to record plant design]	Outlines the requirements to take records on plant that requires registration inc. risk controls, and the requirement to provide this information to the manufacturer	No mention of AI / Robots	Registered AI / Robots will require similar records and specifications of controls used to minimise risk	The specifications for plant outlined in this section should be separately applied to AI / Robots
S237 – Records of plant	Outlines additional requirements to record tests, inspections, maintenance, de/commission, dismantling, and alterations of registered plant	No mention of AI / Robots	Registered AI / Robot systems will require records to be taken for all actions listed under this section	The specifications for plant outlined in this section should be separately applied to AI / Robots
S238 – Operation of amusement devices	Outlines the requirements for amusement devices to be tested without participants under the supervision of a competent person in a manner that does not pose a risk to health and safety	No mention of AI / Robots	It is conceivable that AI / Robotic systems could be used as entertainment/amusement devices. The relevant risks to persons interacting with these AIs must be controlled	Depending on the nature of the device (i.e., robot dancers) it is likely that the list of risks will need to include other considerations such as risk of "amusement AI" malfunction, ethical concerns, and potential psychosocial effects

S243 - Plant design to be registered	Schedule 5 lists the elements of plant design to be registered in accordance with this section of the Regulations	No mention of AI / Robots	Certain intelligent AI / Robotic systems will undoubtedly require registration under new criteria than is currently available under Schedule 5 (officer AIs)	The list under Schedule 5 should be expanded to include a number of potential AI / Robotic systems inc. monitoring AIs, AIs that perform hazardous manual tasks, and AIs that may have authority over the workplace
S244 - Altered plant designs to be registered	Outlines the specifications for alterations to plant to be registered under Schedule 5	No mention of AI / Robots	Alterations to AI systems / robotics will also be registered	A determination of what alterations it is acceptable to make to certain classes of AI systems should be made to prevent possibility of malfunction
S251 - Design verification statement	Outlines the qualifications required for the person who signs the design verification statement	Currently no listed require-ment for AI systems to receive a design verification statement	Safe AI systems will require verification	Language in this section can remain the same
S252 - Who can be the design verifier	Outlines the qualifications required for the person who can verify plant designs	Currently no listed require-ment for AI designed systems to be verified	AI / Robotic systems will need to have their designed verified by a competent person before they can be used in the workplace	Language in this section can remain the same
S267 - When is a person compe-tent to inspect plant	Outlines the qualifications required for the person who can inspect plant	Currently no listed require-ment for AI systems to be inspected	AI / Robotic systems will need to be routinely inspected to ensure it is operating correctly	Language in this section can remain the same

| Continued

Section	Description	Currently	AI / Robots	Commentary
S300 – Compliance with safe work method statement [For high-risk construction]	Outlines the requirement for the PCBU to carry out high-risk construction work in accordance with the safe work method statement	Currently no requirement to include AI systems into safe work method statement	AI / Robots (particularly those engaged in high-risk construction work) will need to be included in Safe Work Method Statements	Safe Work Method Statements should include sections for managing the risk of AI / Robots. The language in this section can remain the same
S315 – Further health and safety duties -specific risks	Outlines specific health & safety duties with regards to disposal of substances or plant, as well as storage	There are no specifications regarding the storage of or robots / AI system when not in use	When not in use or operational, it is expected that robots will need to be stored	This section should be expanded to include the storage of AI systems / robots
S316 – Duty to provide general construction induction training	Outlines the PCBU's duty to provide training and induction to workers expected to carry out general construction tasks	Does not consider AI / Robot trainers. Does not consider methods to train AI/robots in general construction	Robots / AIs may be able to have essential training data uploaded into them, qualifying them for the task	Consideration should be made for the role of workplace training AIs as well as the ability to program AIs with new training behaviours. It is possible that this may count as a change in design.
S317 - Duty to ensure worker has been trained	Outlines the PCBU's duty to ensure workers have received adequate training and holds a training card	Does not consider AI / Robot trainers. Does not consider methods to train AI / robots	Electronic workers may be more easily trained in hazardous tasks compared to human personnel	It may be necessary to consider certain tasks that are considerably high-risk to only be performed by trained AI / robot work groups
S326 - Duties of workers	Outlines the requirements for workers to have a general construction training card and a training certificate	Does not consider AI/Robots	Electronic persons would be expected to hold the same duties under this section, though they may not be required to carry physical cards	The language in this section can remain unchanged

S359 - Fire protection requirement of and firefighting equipment	Outlines the requirement of the PCBU to have fire protection that is appropriate for the workplace	Does not consider role of AI / Robots in combat fire hazards	Specialised AI / Robotic systems can be used to combat fire hazards	Requirement for "fire-fighting" robots / AIs in workplaces that are at a high risk of the occurrence of a fire
S420 - Exposure to airborne asbestos at workplace	Outlines the requirement to consider limit exposure of asbestos to workers as far as is reasonably practicable	Does not consider the role of AI / Robots in asbestos removal	Robots can be expected to be unharmed by asbestos – may be utilised for all asbestos removal tasks in the future due to minimal risk	Requirement for specialised robots to perform asbestos removal tasks to ensure that human workers are not unnecessarily exposed
S703 – Primary duty of care [to general public]	Outlines the requirement for the PCBU to ensure the health and safety of any persons who may be affected by the actions of the PCBU	Does not consider the risk of AI / Robots to interact with the general public	Workplace AIs / Robots could potentially interact with members of the general public	All AI / Robotic systems that may come into contact with the general public must be determined to be safe before it can be allowed to operate in proximity to the general public
S705 – Duties of other persons at relevant premises	Outlines the requirements for other persons to take care for their health and safety	Does not consider the risk of AI / Robots to the general public	Other persons may wish to interact with AI / Robots despite not being safe	Any AI / Robotic system that could cause harm to other persons should have necessary safeguards

Liam Kelly of Manage Damage created this table, which highlights the current shortfalls of today's guides and Codes of Practice to acknowledge Artificial Intelligence and Humanoid Robotics in the Workplace. The Guidance on the Principles of Safe Design for work has been developed by the Safe Work Australia and is a guide for all Australian Designers.

SECTION	DESCRIPTION	SHORTFALL FOR AI	ISSUES	RECOMMENDATIONS AND SOLUTIONS
1.1 What is Safe Design?	Describes "safe design" as "the integration of hazard identification and risk assessment methods early in the design process to eliminate or minimise the risks of injury throughout the life of the product being designed. It encompasses all design including facilities, hardware, systems, equipment, products, tooling, materials, energy controls, layout, and configuration"	Does not address safety in AI / Robotics design	The area of AI / Robotics will pose its own set of unique risks that must be controlled. Currently there is little guidance on the management and control of risks associated with AI	Include specification for software i.e.: "It encompasses all design including facilities, hardware, software, systems, equipment," Include any other unique specifications to AI / Robotics including parameters regarding initial programming / design safety
1.5 Legal Obligations	Specifies that there are specific duties that apply to: • designers of plant, buildings and structures • building owners and persons with control of workplaces • manufacturers, importers and suppliers of plant and substances, and • persons who install, erect or modify plant.	Does not address specific legal obligations pertaining to AI / Robotics; currently only addresses plant	The legal requirements specified for plant are expected to be similar to AI requirements with additional specifications regarding the safe design of intelligent computer systems	• "designers of plant, AI systems, robots, building and structures" • building owners and persons with control of workplaces • manufacturers, importers and suppliers of plant and substances, and • manufacturers, importers and suppliers of AI systems and robots • persons who install, erect or modify plant. • persons who install or modify AI systems or robots

2.1 Persons with Control	Outlines the responsibilities of the persons with control, particularly in making design decisions through-out the product's lifetime and alterations in design	Does not consider what consti-tutes an alteration in the design of an AI / Robot	Machine learning AI systems that learn from the environment may register any constant alterations to design – some of which could negatively affect it	A requirement (as stated in the Regulations) to register any alterations to the design of AI / robotic systems – possibly through constant monitoring of AI / Robot behaviour
2.2 Product Lifecycle	Outlines the expected lifecycle of a product as including: • constructed or manufactured • imported, supplied or installed • commissioned, used or operated • maintained, repaired, cleaned, and/or • modified • de-commis-sioned, demolished and/or • dismantled, and/or • disposed of or recycled.	Does not consider whether how this product lifecycle may apply to AI / Robotic systems	Must consider whether there are any ethical implications in the decommission/dis-mantling of sufficiently intelligent AI systems and whether PCBUs are obligated to treat "injuries" to AI / Robotic systems as they would be for a worker Must also consider retrieval of sensitive information from dismantled robots / AI	Potentially unique requirements regarding the lifecycle of AI systems should be examined with consideration to privacy and ethical concerns
2.2.2 Design	Includes considera-tion towards a number of aspects in design including: • Design for safe erection and installation • Design to facilitate safe use • Physical characteristics of users • Consider intended use and reasonably foreseeable misuse • Design so the plant fails to safety	Does not include design consider-ation specifi-cally for AI / Robots	The considerations that must be made under this section largely apply to AI / Robotic systems as well. In particular, methods to ensure the "safe" failure of an AI / Robot system could prevent potential incidents	Plant design considerations for this section should be adapted and applied to AI / Robotics

2.2.3 Construction and Manufacturing	Includes requirements for constructors and manufacturers to follow design plans as well as to include plans and schedules which ensure safe construction and manufacturing constructor's risk assessments and OHS management systems	Does not specify requirements for safe construction / manufacture of AI / Robotic systems	Currently unclear what the necessary relationship will be between hardware and software for AI & Robotics – designers and manufacturers may operate in completely different areas compared to plant development	Construction and manufacturing considerations for this section should be adapted and applied to AI / Robotics
2.2.4 Supply and Installation	"Suppliers should also conduct risk assessments for the safe receipt, storage and handling of products. Risk assessments should be based on information provided by designers and manufacturers on the residual risk and risk control measures, whether the products come from within Australia or from overseas."	Does not include supply and installation specifications for AI /Robots	Suppliers of AI/Robotic systems will be expected to have an understanding of the risks involved in their storage and handling.	Ways to effectively perform risk assessments on AI/Robotic units will need to be explored to allow for suppliers to be informed regarding the state of AI / Robots being supplied
2.2.5 - Commission and Usage	States that "person with control of the workplace needs to assess and control the risks that may arise during the operation and use of products"	Does not include specifications for the commission and usage of AI / Robots	Person with control of the workplace needs to be aware of the relevant risks of their AI or robotics systems	Needs to incorporate AI safety into Safe Work Method Statements, Management Systems, and Risk Assessments
2.3.1 Risk Management Process	• identify design-related hazards associated with the range of intended uses, including any foreseeable misuse of the product • assess the risks	Does not specify actions to take regarding the risk management of	One of the reasons that AI systems / Robots may be more likely to be classified as "workers" is because the spectrum of risk that they represent will	The language in this section may stay the same for the most part – however, the process of risk management for sufficiently advanced AI

		AI / Robots	become much more like a human i.e., somewhat unpredictable in nature.	units would be expected to be very difficult as these systems may have very diverse functions that could represent risks in many areas to the point that it would almost be impossible to effectively recognize and manage them all without assistance.
	arising from design-related hazards • eliminate hazards and control risks • monitor and review the risk control measures • maintain records of risk assessments • consult with individuals or groups involved in the lifecycle of the product, and • provide informa-tion on the intended use of products for the benefit of users throughout the product lifecycle."			
2.3.1.1 Identify Hazards	Relevant sections include: • Hazards relating to the products themselves. • Hazards relating to how the products will be used and the environment where they will be used	Does not specify methods to identify hazards that relate to AI / Robots	Certain Robots / AIs could be influenced by the environment and this could have negative conse-quences unless new technologies are invented that can accurately monitor and diagnose potential defects in AI systems before they manifest behaviourally.	Development of methods to monitor AI behaviour and diagnose any potential issues.
2.3.2.7 Commu-nicate and Docu-ment	Outlines the requirements for duty holders to communicate and document relative actions during each design phase and following any alterations	Does not specify require-ments to require-ments to commu-nicate and docu-ment informa-tion that is specific to AI / Robots	Machine-learning AIs can be unpredictable and difficult to monitor (with current technologies). To counteract potential for risk it is important that any relevant informa-tion regarding AI / Robots be stored and made available to other duty holders	The guidelines should be updated to include potent ways to ensure that AIs are operating correctly AI/Robotics will need to be closely monitored and any aberrant or unusual behaviour must be effectively documented and assessed for potential risk

| 2.5.1 - Consultation | Outlines the requirement for duty holders to consult regarding design decisions concerning plant, workplace layout, work systems, etc. | Does not specify requirements to consult with regards to design phases of AI systems /alterations to design | Considering the potential wide variety of risks associated with certain AI/Robotic systems, new specialized areas of "AI consultation" will likely arise, where qualified people can diagnose and manage potential issues with AI systems. | esigners and manufacturers of AI systems & robots will need to be available for continuous consultation at any stage of the lifecycle of the AI system or robot, and should be able to recognize the hallmarks of risk during any of the development stages. |

APPENDIX

RESOURCES

References for Risk Dollarisation®

Resources

Abbot, R., Bogenschneider, B. N. (2017). Should Robots Pay Taxes? Tax Policy in the Age of Automation. Harvard Law & Policy Review, Forthcoming. Retrieved from https://www.roboticsbusinessreview.com/wp-content/uploads/2018/05/Should-Robots-Pay-Taxes.pdf

ACC (2018). ACC Levy Guidebook Your guide to 2017/18 levy rates, industry classifications and invoices. Retrieved from https://www.acc.co.nz/assets/business/acc7686-acc-levy-guidebook-2017-2018.pdf

Adams, R. L. (2017, January 10). 10 Powerful Examples Of Artificial Intelligence In Use Today. Forbes. Retrieved from https://www.forbes.com/sites/robertadams/2017/01/10/10-powerful-examples-of-artificial-intelligence-in-use-today/#614c6fd4420d

Ahlstrom. (2018, 24 May). Chart: Why Industrial Robot Sales are Sky High. Retrieved from http://www.visualcapitalist.com/industrial-robot-sales-sky-high/

Arthur, Don. (2016, 18 November) Basic income: a radical idea enters the mainstream. Retrieved from https://www.aph.gov.au/About_Parliament/Parliamentary_Departments/Parliamentary_Library/pubs/rp/rp1617/BasicIncome

Australian Bureau of Statistics (ABS) (2018, May 26). 2017-18 Key Industry Points. Retrieved from http://www.abs.gov.au/AUSSTATS/abs@.nsf/DetailsPage/6291.0.55.001May%202018?OpenDocument

Australian Bureau of Statistics, (2006). 1292.0 - Australian and New Zealand Standard Industrial Classification (ANZSIC), 2006 (Revision 1.0). Retrieved by http://www.abs.gov.au/AUSSTATS/abs@.nsf/DetailsPage/1292.02006%20(Revision%202.0)?OpenDocument

Australian Safety and Compensation Council. (2006) Guidance on the Principles of Safe Design for Work May 2006 Retrieved from https://www.safeworkaustralia.gov.au/system/files/documents/1702/guidanceontheprinciplesofsafedesign_2006_pdf.pdf

Automous Next Augmented Finance & Machine (2018 April) How Artificial Intelligence creates $1 trillion of change in the front, middle and back office of the financial services industry, what is driving the resurgence of the technology, and where it is going in the future. Retrieved from https://next.autonomous.com/augmented-finance-machine-intelligence/

Awais, M & Henrich, D (2012, May). Online intention learning for human-robot interaction by scene observation https://www.researchgate.net/publication/241631479_Online_intention_learning_for_human-robot_interaction_by_scene_observation

Berger, T., Frey C. B., & Osbourne, M., (2015). Technology at Work: The Future of Innovation and Employment. Citi Research & Oxford Martin School. Retrieved from https://www.oxfordmartin.ox.ac.uk/downloads/reports/Citi_GPS_Technology_Work.pdf

Bogost, I., (2017, July). Why Zuckerberg and Musk Are Fighting About the Robot Future. The Atlantic. Retrieved from: https://www.theatlantic.com/technology/archive/2017/07/musk-vs-zuck/535077/

CB Insights. (2018) The State of Artificial Intelligence 2018. Retrieved from https://www.cbinsights.com/reports/CB-Insights_State-AI-2018-Briefing.pdf

Connor, N. (2017, August 4). Legal Robots Deployed in China to help decide thousands of cases. The Telegraph. Retrieved from https://www.telegraph.co.uk/news/2017/08/04/legal-robots-deployed-china-help-decide-thousands-cases/

Frey, C. B., Osbourne, M., & Holmes, C. (2017). Technology at Work v2.0 The Future is Not What it Used To Be. Citi Research & Oxford Martin School. Retrieved from https://www.oxfordmartin.ox.ac.uk/downloads/reports/Citi_GPS_Technology_Work_2.pdf

European Committee on Legal Affairs (2016). Commission on Civil Law rules on Robotics. Retrieved from http://www.europarl.europa.eu/sides/getDoc.do?pubRef=-//EP//NONSGML%2BCOMPARL%2BPE-582.443%2B01%2BDOC%2BPDF%2BV0//EN

Garfield, L. (2016, March 2). 7 companies that are replacing human jobs with robots. Business Insider. Retrieved from http://www.businessinsider.com/companies-that-use-robots-instead-of-humans-2016-2?IR=T#quiet-logistics-robots--quickly-find-package-and-ship-online-orders-in-warehouses-2

Gibbs, Samuel (2018, 19 April). Tesla factory to be investigated over safety concerns. Retrieved from https://www.theguardian.com/technology/2018/apr/19/tesla-california-factory-investigated-safety-concerns-model-3

Hanson Robotics (2018). Sophia. Retrieved from http://www.hansonrobotics.com/robot/sophia/

Harris, Ainsley (2018, 5 August) AI Could Kill 2.5 Million Financial Jobs—And Save Banks $1 Trillion Retrieved from https://www.fastcompany.com/40568069/ai-could-kill-2-5-million-financial-jobs-and-save-banks-1-trillion?utm_source=postup&utm_medium=email&utm_campaign=Fast

Hern, A. (2017, September). Elon Musk says AI could lead to third world war. The Guardian. Retrieved from https://www.theguardian.com/technology/2017/sep/04/elon-musk-ai-third-world-war-vladimir-putin

Horton, J, Cameron A, Davaraj D, Hanson RT, Hajkowicz SA, CSIRO. (2018) Workplace Safety Futures: The Impact of emerging technologies and platforms on work health and safety on workers compensation over the next twenty years. Retrieved from https://www.data61.csiro.au/en/Our-Work/Future-Cities/Planning-sustainable-infrastructure/WorkplaceSafety

International Social Security Association (2017, 2 September) Report on Work Reintegration. Retrieved from https://www.issa.int/en/details?uuid=f8ded415-513e-4326-9ecf-00231eb2a279

International Labour Organisation (2018). Safety and Health at Work. Retrieved from http://www.ilo.org/global/topics/safety-and-health-at-work/lang--en/index.htm

International Labour Organisation (2018). Improving the Safety and Health of Young Workers. Retrieved from http://www.ilo.org/wcmsp5/groups/public/---ed_protect/---protrav/---safework/documents/publication/wcms_625223.pdf

International Monetary Fund (April 2018)World Economic and Financial Surveys and Outlook Database Retrieved from http://www.imf.org/ http://statisticstimes.com/economy/countries-by-projected-gdp.php

Institute for Work and Health (2009) Workers' Compensation and the Business Cycle – Issue Briefing, Institute for Work and Health, March, Toronto. Retrieved from https://www.iwh.on.ca/summaries/issue-briefing/workers-compensation-and-business-cycle

McKinsey & Company. (2017, December) Jobs Lost, Jobs Gained: Workforce Transitions. Retrieved from https://www.mckinsey.com/~/media/McKinsey/Featured%20Insights/Future%20of%20Organizations/What%20the%20future%20of%20work%20will%20mean%20for%20jobs%20skills%20and%20wages/MGI-Jobs-Lost-Jobs-Gained-Report-December-6-2017.ashx

Miller, Jason (2014). The Right Brain vs. Left Brain of Marketers [Infographic]. Retrieved from https://blog.marketo.com/2012/01/the-right-brain-vs-left-brain-of-marketers.html

Narrative Science & National Business Research Institute (2016). Outlook of Artificial Intelligence in the Enterprise 2016. Retrieved from https://narrativescience.com/Portals/0/Images/PDFs/OutlookOnAI2018_NarrativeScience.pdf

News Corp Australia Network. (2017, October 30). Saudi Arabia gives a robot citizenship in world first. The New York Post. Retrieved from https://www.news.com.au/technology/innovation/inventions/saudi-arabia-gives-a-robot-citizenship-in-world-first/news-story/c46db098b973544aabd0fb1827c27114

O'Neill, M. (2017, August 7). Explainer: What is artificial intelligence? ABC News. Retrieved from http://www.abc.net.au/news/2017-08-07/explainer-what-is-artificial-intelligence/8771632

Pricewaterhousecooper [PwC] (2017). Sizing the Prize: What's the real value of AI for your business and how can you capitalize? Retrieved from: https://www.pwc.com/gx/en/issues/analytics/assets/pwc-ai-analysis-sizing-the-prize-report.pdf

Safe Work Australia. (2017, March) Measuring and reporting on work health and safety. Retrieved from https://www.safeworkaustralia.gov.au/doc/measuring-and-reporting-work-health-and-safety

Sanchez, D. (2017, January 20). Automation and the World of Workers' Comp. On-site Physio. Retrieved from: http://www.onsite-physio.com/reports/automation-and-the-world-of-workers-comp

Sohrabi-Shiraz, Ariane (2018, 9 January). Sex robot maker Sergi Santos: Who is he and what does Synthea Amatus do? Retrieved from https://www.dailystar.co.uk/news/latest-news/672709/sex-robot-Sergi-Santos-who-is-sex-robot-news-Synthea-Amatus-Samantha-doll-Barcelona

Taylor, Michael (2018, 22 March). Fatal Uber Crash Was 'Inevitable,' Says BMW's Top Engineer

Retrieved from https://www.forbes.com/sites/michaeltaylor/2018/03/22/fatal-uber-crash-inevitable-says-bmws-top-engineer/#7d6543d55688

Tegmark, M. (2016). Benefits & Risks of Artificial Intelligence. Future of Life. Retrieved from https://futureoflife.org/background/benefits-risks-of-artificial-intelligence/?cn-reloaded=1

Texile Industry Sustainability Forum (2016, October) Calculating the Return on Prevention for Companies, Costs and Benefits of Investments in Occupational Safety and Health in Pakistan's Textile and Garment Sector. Retrieved from http://ciwce.org.pk/wp-content/uploads/2017/09/ROP-Report_web.pdf

United Kingdom, House of Commons. (2017, 26 April) United Kingdom Self-Employment and the Gig Economy May 2017 Retrieved from https://publications.parliament.uk/pa/cm201617/cmselect/cmworpen/847/847.pdf

Ward, Susan. (2018, 11 June). Guide to Workers' Compensation in Canada for Businesses. Retrieved from https://www.thebalancesmb.com/guide-to-workers-compensation-insurance-2947112

Wolfe, A. (2017). Unstoppable? The gap between public safety and traffic safety in the age of driverless cars. Calhoun Institutional Archive of the Naval Postgraduate School. Retrieved from https://calhoun.nps.edu/bitstream/handle/10945/52952/17Mar_Wolfe_Aristotle.pdf?sequence=1&isAllowed=y

Workcover Queensland Gazette Notice Workers' Compensation and Rehabilitation Act 2003 (Q) WorkCover Queensland Notice (No. 1) of 2018. Retrieved from https://www.worksafe.qld.gov.au/__data/assets/pdf_file/0020/8057/Queensland-Government-Gazette.pdf

Workplace Health & Safety Act 2011 (Qld). Retrieved from https://www.legislation.qld.gov.au/view/html/inforce/current/act-2011-018

Workplace Health & Safety Regulation 2011 (Qld). Retrieved from https://www.legislation.qld.gov.au/view/html/inforce/current/sl-2011-0240

Workplace Health and Safety Queensland (2013, February). Construction Industry Report, Information and Evaluation Unit, WHSQ Retrieved from https://www.worksafe.qld.gov.au/__data/assets/pdf_file/0019/83206/report-construction-industry.pdf

World in Figures by The Economist. (2018). Retrieved from https://worldinfigures.com

Conference Board CEO C-Suite ChallengeTM (2018, 18 January). Global Survey of C-Suite: Recession Fears Fade, But Talent Concerns Remain. Retrieved from https://www.prnewswire.com/news-releases/global-survey-of-c-suite-recession-fears-fade-but-talent-concerns-remain-300584459.html

APPENDIX

GLOSSARY

Definitions for Risk Dollarisation®

Glossary

AI	Artificial Intelligence
Applied AI	Applied AIs use machine learning to learn and adapt without needing to be programmed. On the net these AIs watch your activity and use it to make new suggestions. Applied AI can also be combined with sensors to create machines that can learn from the environment.
Artificial Intelligence	A computer system that can think, learn, and adapt based on user and environmental input; or A computer system that can perform tasks that humans would require intelligence to do.
Contributory Principle	Contributory Principle, "a social contract between individuals and the state" that is central to many countries' welfare systems.
Damage	Loss or harm resulting from injury to person, property, or reputation
Damages	Compensation in money imposed by law for loss or injury (in the legal field)
Damage Costs	The cost incurred by repercussions (effects) of direct environmental impacts (for example, from the emission of pollutants) such as the degradation of land or human-made structures and health effects. In environmental accounting, it is part of the costs borne by economic agents. It should be noted the concept is not primarily focused on "damages" in the above legal sense (See definition: Damages). Whilst damages of this nature are included in The Financial Approach to Non-Financial Risk, it is essential that the focus is on avoidance of damage, which in turn results in avoidance of damages. The word "damage" is chosen and used to speak to the commercial/business/operational parties of a business whom regularly speak in these terms for stock and accounts of widgets (See definition: Widgets) worldwide.

Damage Costs are all those costs associated with harm in a business environment. Environment" should be taken broadly as the OECD approaches as the whole operation and the environment in which it operates.

The words and phrases are to frame a commercial approach to risk and its management in terms business owners know, understand and are comfortable to operate within.

Damage Cost Assessment	A financial assessment of a business Damage Costs.
Damage Cost Black Holes	Where money apparently disappears without a trace.
Electronic Person	Creating a specific legal status for robots, so that at least the most sophisticated autonomous robots could be established as having the status of electronic persons with specific rights and obligations, including that of making good any damage they may cause, and applying electronic personality to cases where robots make smart autonomous decisions or otherwise interact with third parties independently.
Financial Risk	Any of the various types of risk associated with financing, including financial transactions that include company loans in risk of default. Often it is understood to include only downside risk, meaning the potential for financial loss and uncertainty about its extent:

Credit Risk

- Market Risk

- Interest Rate Risk in the Banking Book

- Liquidity Risk

Gazette	An official journal, a newspaper of record, or simply a newspaper.

In English- and French-speaking countries, newspaper publishers have applied the name Gazette since the 17th century; today, numerous weekly and daily newspapers bear the name The Gazette.

Generalised AI   Generalised AI are AIs with human or above intelligence that can perform any task. They do not currently exist, but leading experts believe it may be on the horizon.

Hard and Soft Science   Colloquial terms used to compare scientific fields on the basis of perceived methodological rigor, exactitude and objectivity.

Roughly speaking, the natural sciences are considered "hard", whereas the social sciences are usually described as "soft".

Humanoid Robot or "Humanoids"   Something that resembles or looks like a human and having characteristics like opposable thumb, ability to walk in upright position, etc.

In general they have a torso with a head, two arms and two legs, although some forms of humanoid robots may model only part of the body, for example, from the waist up. Some may also have a 'face', with 'eyes' and 'mouth'. Androids are humanoid robots built to resemble a male human, and Gynoids are humanoid robots built to resemble a human female. A Humanoid robot is fully automated as it can adapt to its surroundings and continue with its goals.

ILO   International Labour Organisation

Industry Rate   Industry Rate is the average or commencement rate that is applied to a particular Workers Compensation Code

ISSA   International Social Security Association

Kairotic moment   Kairos in Ancient Greek meant "time"; the exact right time to say or do a particular thing. It refers to making exactly the right statement at exactly the right moment.

LTIFR   Lost Time Injury Frequency Rate

Market Driven Theory Approach   Poses the question of the relationship between markets and competitive advantage.

Market-driven firms reveal a superior ability to understand, attract and maintain a supply of products/services that offer more value for the customer than competitors.

The Resource-Based Theory originates from Penrose's idea (1959) of the firm as a coordinated 'bundle' of resources that the business has at its disposal or has access to (inside out), which are valuable, rare and inimitable.

In global markets, MDM strives towards continuous innovation processes that can enable the company to escape the potential pressure of the competition, by identifying new customer needs to satisfy (outside in).

The market-driven company is not only oriented to the market, but also tends to orient the market.

Resource-Based Theory and Market-Driven

Non-Financial Risk	Non-Financial Risk is those items of risk that are not normally managed in monetary or financially reported:

- Operational Risk
- Compliance Risk
- Conduct Risk
- IT Risk
- Cyber Risk
- Third- Party Risk

Profit	A financial gain, especially the difference between the amount earned and the amount spent in buying, operating, or producing something.
Qualitative	Relating to, measuring, or measured by the quality of something rather than its quantity.
	Adjective: the quality of something in size, appearance, value, etc. Such adjectives can be submodified by words such as very and have comparative and superlative forms.
Quantitative	Relating to, measuring, or measured by the quantity of something rather than its quality.
	i.e. "quantitative analysis"

Relative	Considered in relation to or in proportion to something else
ROI	Return on Investment
Return on Investment	Return on Investment (ROI) is a performance measure used to evaluate the efficiency of an investment or to compare the efficiency of a number of different investments. ROI measures the amount of return on an investment, relative to the investment's cost.
ROP	Return on Prevention
Soft Science	See: "Hard and Soft Science"
TRIFR	Total Recordable Injury Frequency Rate
UBI	A universal basic income (UBI) is a payment made to all adult individuals that allows people to meet their basic needs. It is made without any work or activity tests.

There are a number of different UBI models. These range from more modest schemes designed to simplify the existing social security system all the way to utopian plans to transform society. |
| **Widgets** | Economists often use the term widget to refer to an abstract unit of production. Factories produce widgets using capital and labour. |

ACKNOWLEDGMENTS
YOU KNOW WHO YOU ARE

Remain #EPIC I am externally grateful

The Husband - The Accountant - The Farmer

The Wonder Woman - The Elon - The SuzeZ - The Ginger

APPENDIX
ABOUT THE AUTHOR

Biography

J L HAMILTON

Jillian Hamilton is the Managing Director of Manage Damage, an Australian risk management advisory firm. As a well-known speaker and mentor, Jillian's great ability to form positive relationships has made her known throughout the entrepreneurial world for being a strong and insightful business leader.

Following her extensive career across many industries, Jillian saw the need to approach safety and risk in a different way. Her vast knowledge on health and safety has seen many businesses save millions of dollars in Damage Costs. Currently studying a Bachelor of Laws, Jillian's impressive academic background consists of a Post Graduate Diploma in Occupational Health, Safety and the Environment and a Bachelor in Natural Resource Economics. Jillian has studied the complete set of key skill sets for risk, ranging from ergonomics, to economics to ecometrics, to environmental law and politics.

As a result of Jillian's hard-working ethos, Manage Damage has been successful with both public and private sectors. The business works from a holistic perspective by understanding clients' needs and providing value with every offering. This was demonstrated when Manage Damage was awarded the Risk Management

Advisory Firm of the Year in 2017, Most Outstanding Risk Management Advisory Firm of the Year 2018, 2018 Gold Stevie Award for Product Innovation for HR and 2018 Gold Stevie Award for Product Innovation for a Business to Business Service.

When asked what Jillian's philosophy for life is, she remarked, "We get one shot at life and living and I want to say that if I died tomorrow I had no regrets, I tried everything and didn't leave any stones unturned. There are so many amazing places and people in this world – I look forward to seeing as many people and places as I can." This is shown by the list of places she has visited, career highlights and achievements, and has contributed to Jillian appearing on radio, winning awards and speaking at many events.

As a well-connected inspirational game changer, whose mission is to raise the profile on risk and safety within the workplace, Jillian's one goal is to make customers self-sustainable so that they can stand on their own as soon as possible. Her strong leadership skills and innovative ideas have led to her to quickly become a valued thought leader within the industry.

APPENDIX
APPEARANCES

Speaking Appearances & Articles with JL Hamilton

NSCA
National Safety Council of Australia

ClubsNSW

SAFETY 2018
CONNECT
Incorporating the National Safety Conference

NMW
NATIONAL MANUFACTURING WEEK

IAIABC
Find Information. Connect People.

LIQUID
LEARNING
bebetter

RECRUITMENT
YARNS
LEARN SHARE THRIVE

AMIC

marcusevans

XXI WORLD CONGRESS ON
SAFETY & HEALTH
AT WORK 2017
3-6 September 2017
Sands Expo and Convention Centre, Singapore

CFC INNOVATION

Talkers
BusinessRadio

NSW REGIONAL
SAFETY
CONFERENCE & EXPO
2018

safety
in action

101 fm
it's all about the music !

Lawyers
McCullough
Robertson

giz
Deutsche Gesellschaft
für Internationale
Zusammenarbeit (GIZ) GmbH

ILO
International
Labour
Organization

CommonwealthBank

RecTech
SOLUTIONS

BEEF AUSTRALIA 2021 ROCKHAMPTON

S.I.A.
Safety Institute of Australia

LAGOS VISION ZERO
Safety. Health. Wellbeing

QUEENSLAND
Country Life

THE LAND

VISIONS
conference

VISION ZERO
Safety.Health.Wellbeing.

eIMEX
GUNNEDAH
energy Innovation
Mining Expo

ESSI
PUNJAB

- **October 2014** - 4th Annual National Safety Psychology Conference 2014 - "No Resilience – Uh That's Going to Hurt You" - Liquid Learning www.liquidlearning.com.au

- **November 2014** - Beyond Zero Harm: Human Factor Safety Melbourne – "Zero Cost for Zero Harm - Humanising impacts in safety operations to reengineer safety approach for enhanced productivity and business profitability" - Marcus Evans www.marcusevans.com

- **October 2015** - 6th Annual SIA NT Work Health and Safety Conference – "No Resilience - That's Going to Cost You! & Rehabilitation and Return to Work Master Class" - Safety Institute of Australia www.sia.org.au

- **November 2015** - Safety: The Next Frontier Conference Melbourne, Australia – "Safety as Survival – Inuit Instinct and Safety in Practice" - Marcus Evans www.marcusevans.com

- **January 2017** - Radio Interview, Brisbane Australia – "Manage Damage & Climbing Everest" – 101FM - http://www.101fm.com.au

- **May 2017** – Safety First Expo/National Manufacturing Week – "Understanding the financial relevance of safe work practices - Accounting for the costs of hurting people" http://www.nationalmanufacturingweek.com.au & http://safetyfirstexpo.com.au

- **May, June, August 2017** - Manage Damage, McCullough Robertson and Allegiant IRS delivered a three part Insurance Coverage Think Tank Series. Bringing leading industry minds together to workshop issues around insurance coverage, identifying and filling gaps in insurance cover, emerging trends and issues in insurance, getting value from insurance and strategies for managing claims.

- **June 2017** - Radio Interview, Brisbane Australia – "Creating A Financial Relevance" – 101FM - http://www.101fm.com.au

- **June 2017** - Recruitment Yarns NZ Auckland and Christchurch – "How to Minimise Workers Compensation Premiums" - http://www.recruitmentyarns.com

- **July 2017** - Australian Meat Industry Council (AMIC) National Meat Industry Work, Health and Safety Conference, Australia's – "'Zero Cost for Zero Harm – Reshifting the focus of Risk to the bottom line" - http://www.amic.org.au

- **August 2017** - Clubs NSW Conference - "Understanding the Financial Relevance of Your Workcover Premiums & How You Can Positively Influence the Price." - http://www.clubsnsw.com.au

- **September 2017** - XXI World Congress on Safety & Health at Work 2017 - The World Congress on Safety and Health at Work opens its doors every three years. Each time, a different country is the host; Sponsored by International Labour Organisation, the International Social Security Association and the Singapore Ministry of Manpower – "Prevention pays! The role of accident insurance and the return to work reintegration" - https://www.safety2017singapore.com/symposia/

- **September 2017** – Newspaper Article - CFO Innovation – Manage Damage Reveals New Solution Global Worker Risk - https://www.cfoinnovation.com/story/13585/manage-damage-reveals-new-solution-global-worker-risk

- **March 2018** – Co-Host Webinar - Rectech Solutions – How to Navigate Workers Compensation Premiums for Labour Hire - Webinars provide up-to-date, insider views on the state of Recruitment Technology and Best Practice - http://www.rectechsolutions.com.au/events/free-webinars/

- **March 2018** - NSW Regional Safety and Conference and Expo 2018 - Creating A Financial Relevance http://nswsafetyconference.com.au

- **April 2018** - Breakfast Seminar - Brooke Jacobs & McCullough Robertson Lawyers - Managing Workers' Compensation Claims – From incident through to claim resolution - http://www.mccullough.com.au/events-directory/

- **April 2018** - International Workshop – International Workshop on Safety Practices and Issues – Pakistan – "Gig/Informal Economy and the Challenges of New Age Work" https://vimeo.com/268725023

- **April 2018** - World Day for Safety and Health at Work - This year, the World Day for Safety and Health at Work (SafeDay) and the World Day Against Child Labour (WDACL) are coming together in a joint campaign to improve the safety and health of young workers and end child labour - Pakistan – "Return on Investment- A Financial Approach To Work Place Injuries and Reducing Damage Costs. https://vimeo.com/271067497

- **May 2018** – Expo - BeefWeek 2018 - Australia's national beef expo is one of the world's great beef cattle events and is held just once every three years in Rockhampton, Queensland, Australia – "Risk Dollarisation® and the Financial Approach to Non-Financial Risk" – http://beefaustralia.com.au

- **May 2018** – Newspaper Article – The Land & The Queensland Country Life - Beef producers taking a big hit from WorkCover premiums - Beef farmers are the "yellow V8 driving 18-year-olds" when it comes to assessing their WorkCover insurance premiums - https://www.theland.com.au/story/5394201/get-serious-about-the-cost-of-injuries-beef-producers-told/?cs=4933

- **June 2018** – BoardRoom Lunch - Australian Institute of Company Directors Round table discussion on "Risk Dollarisation and the Financial Approach to Non-Financial Risk" – Commonwealth Bank Australia Sponsor http://aicd.companydirectors.com.au

- **June 2018** – Radio Interview – Talkers FM - "Manage Damage : Risk Management to Reduce Damage Costs" - https://talkers.fm/manage-damage-risk-management-to-reduce-damage-costs/

- **June 2018** – Conference - Nigeria Vision Zero Launch – "Risk Dollarization® - Transforming Risk Management where Risk is Quantified in Dollar Terms as a Currency" - www.lagosvisionzero.ng

- **August 2018** – Conference - Safety Governance in Practice World Vision Zero Launch – International Social Security Association (ISSA) presented by Manage Damage & Australian Institute of Company Directors - The ultimate take home message will be that "no-one deserves to be harmed at work" - https://aicd.companydirectors.com.au/events/events-calendar/qld/ev139284-special-events

- **August 2018** - SAFETYconnect 2018 presented by the National Safety Council of Australia (NSCA) - Risk Dollarisation® - http://www.safety-connect.com.au

- **September 2018** – SIA Visions Conference – Safety Institute of Australia (SIA) - Risk Dollarisation® - https://www.visions.org.au

- **October 2018** - IAIABC 104th Convention, Virginia, USA - Panel on "Innovative Approaches to Coverage." - Innovative approaches that are happening in Australia for a 20-30 minute presentation as part of a panel - https://www.iaiabc.org/assnfe/ev.asp?ID=521

- **October 2018** - National Employment Solutions - The Changing Face of Work and the Workplace – "The Gig Economy & Challenges with the New Age Work" - https://www.employmentsolutions.net.au

- **October 2018** - Safety in Action - Minimising the Cost of Work-Related Injuries - Overview of NWC and benefits for injured workers & Reducing costs and improving ROI - https://www.informa.com.au/event/conference/return-work-conference/?_ga=2.219915545.160157300.1531789216-451042183.1531789216

- **November 2018** - Energy, Innovation & Mining Expo (eIMEx) – A Financial Approach to Non-Financial Risk - http://www.gunnedahshowsociety.com.au/events/energy-innovation-mining-expo-eimex/

APPENDIX

AWARDS

Manage Damage® Business Awards

Risk Dollarisation®

June 2017

ACQ5 Global APAC Award 2017

ACQ5 Global Risk Management Advisory Firm of the Year

ACQ Annual Award Programs recognise organisations and individuals that have achieved outstanding commercial success in designated areas of expertise.

http://www.acq5.com/posts/gamechangers/

July 2017

The Gold Award for Business Excellence (Australia)

The Award is run on a State level, and folds into a National Awards program where Gold Awardees become eligible to win the National Gold Award for their category.

http://www.goldaward.biz/pdf/entrykit.pdf

July 2017

The Gold Award for Business Excellence (QLD)

Criteria is awareness of the continual business improvement process and underlying principles for achieving competitiveness and organisational success; and

An understanding of all the requirements for business excellence.

They are based on eight critical Management Systems elements necessary for excellence and sound organisation-wide management.

http://www.goldaward.biz/pdf/entrykit.pdf

March 2018

SmartCompany's International Women's Day Showcase

Women who have inspired, challenged and supported people in their careers. SC believe that increasing the visibility of women and acknowledging the distinct leadership and learning styles they bring will not only produce better business outcomes - it'll lead to us solving some of the biggest issues of our time.

https://www.smartcompany.com.au/iwd/

May 2018

Most Outstanding Risk Management Advisory Firm of the Year - Australia

Honoured to be Awarded the Corporate Excellence Awards 2018 - Most Outstanding Risk Management Advisory Firm of the Year – Australia

https://www.cv-magazine.com/issues/issue-5-2018/37/#zoom=z

June 2018

Award for Innovation in Business-to-Business Services

GOLD STEVIE® WINNER

Manage Damage, Woolloongabba, QLD Australia: Risk Dollarisation –

A Groundbreaking Approach to Non-Financial Risk

http://asia.stevieawards.com/2018-stevie-winners

March 2018

Finalist Anthill Cool Company Awards 2017

Cool Companies manage to stay one step ahead of the rest. They breed leaders who are rule-makers and rule-breakers. They are organisations that aspire to be admired. They are trend-setters in attitude and action. Quite simply, they are... cool!

http://anthillonline.com

July 2018

IAIABC NextGen Award

The IAIABC NextGen seeks to recognize new talent and leadership in workers' compensation as the industry, like many others, moves to adapt and thrive in a changing world. It is a way to recognize the contributions of individuals under the age of 40 working in the workers' compensation industry.

https://www.iaiabc.org/iaiabc/NextGen.asp

June 2018

Award for Innovation in Human Resources Management, Planning & Practice

GOLD STEVIE® WINNER:

Manage Damage, Woolloongabba, QLD Australia: Risk Dollarisation –

A Groundbreaking Approach to Non-Financial Risk

http://asia.stevieawards.com/2018-stevie-winners

APPENDIX
TRADEMARKING & PATENTS

Information on Manage Damage®

Trademarking & Licensing

At least some of the systems and methodologies discussed in this book are the subject of intellectual property rights including patents, trademarks and copyright.

APPENDIX

ADDITIONAL PRODUCTS

Safety Financial Reporting - Damage Cost Reviews - Global Supply Chain Management - Safety in Design - M&A - Other Services

Safety Financial Reporting

MetricDriver® - Non-Financial Risk in a Financial Report

Damage Cost Reviews

Uncover where your business is losing money & how to improve workforce and fiscal health

MANAGE
DAMAGE

Global Supply Chain Management

Risk Reviews, Mapping & Advice
Let us help you navigate the global supply uncharted

Merger & Acquisition Reviews

We assess Damage & Insurance Costs for your impending sale, purchase or merge - implications can be very financial.

MANAGE DAMAGE

Other Services

Safety In Design - AI, Robotics and Other Plant
Legal Compliance Reviews & Due Diligence Reviews
Risk Management Strategic Advice
Futurist Advice

www.managedamage.com

explore@managedamage.com

MANAGE DAMAGE

Manage Damage works with Boards, CEOs, CFOs and other senior leaders to drive efficiency, productivity and profitability by dollarising a business's risk portfolio.

Manage Damage is able to create an environment where non-financial risk is converted into dollar terms to enable management to more easily address the complex interplay of these factors within a business and reduce associated costs.

"Our method provides senior management with risk information in language they understand – we convert non-financial data into a financial context to enable businesses to see where issues lie and where true associated costs are located."

By assessing a company's risk portfolio via the cost of damage they are able to better manage and reduce, the costs associated with risk. We provide complete visibility of true damage costs and highlight the opportunities to manage the damage. Our unique approach to 'dollarising' risk reduces the cost of damage and the negative impact on the bottom-line.

To provide ongoing visibility, accountability and measurement to this area of risk across the entire business we developed MetricDriver™, a powerful process that uses the philosophy of Risk Dollarisation™.

We provide positive impacts and results for Companies - Business Units – Countries - Employer Self Insurers - Employer Funded Insurance – States.

We welcome the opportunity to have a confidential conversation about your risk needs.

Connect with us;

www.managedamage.com

Facebook: ManageDamage

Twitter: @Jillian.Lee.Hamilton

info@managedamage.com

Instagram: Manage_Damage

LinkedIn: https://www.linkedin.com/in/jillianlhamilton/

www.ingramcontent.com/pod-product-compliance
Lightning Source LLC
Chambersburg PA
CBHW042310210326
41598CB00041B/7333

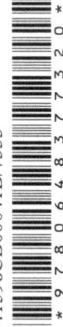